Praise for

Made Competent: A Story about Life in Ministry

It is overwhelming to think about, yet at the same time, a super time to be in ministry. We have the opportunity to be proclaiming the truths of Jesus and the Scriptures to a generation that doesn't know. Casey has written a book here which is so hopeful. It is not just looking at the negative things, but the positive opportunities we have—and practical ways to move forward to see a generation know Jesus and grow in their faith.

—**Dan Kimball**, author of *How (Not) To Read The Bible* and VP of *Western Seminary*

***

In this bravely honest and searching memoir, Casey welcomes us into his journey as a campus minister (something he did not intend to be) with some soaring high points and crushing troughs, both professional and personal. But it is much more than his story… it is his invitation to do your examination of God's work in your own story and a call to all of us to attend to the hundreds of thousands of students on campuses across America… surely one of the primary mission fields in our backyards. READ IT! And along the way write your own story!

—**Randy Harris**, Retired Professor at Abilene Christian University and author of *God Work* and *Living Jesus*

***

In *Made Competent,* Casey Coston has poured his heart and soul out to all of us involved in reaching collegians for Christ. His vision, passion, and years of experience give us a very personal and powerful insight into his life and ministry. You will be challenged to go deeper into your calling and commitment to invest yourself in winning, discipling and launching this incredibly strategic group we call students.
—**Steve Shadrach**, author of *The Fuel and the Flame* and *The God Ask*

***

Feelings of inadequacy and weakness are an everyday part of serving in the ministry. Casey Coston, in his book *Made Competent,* tells his compelling story of moving from inadequacy to confidence. Stories of his many years of serving the Lord on the university campus flow from the pages with transparency and passion. Casey openly shares his victories and challenges as only he can. If you wrestle with things like balancing family and ministry, working more effectively within your leadership structures, or enduring the inevitable seasons of suffering, this book gives you help and hope.
—**Greg Swinney**, General Editor of *The Gospel Goes to College* Vol 1 and 2 and *Taking Education Higher*

***

It's hard to communicate how much I appreciate your story. I feel like I know you so much better. Your heart was intimately revealed. I was impressed with the way you shared all of your struggles and heartaches. I wish you hadn't been burdened with so much pain. I so wish you could have been spared. But as you said--it brought resurrection. I also like the way you stayed true to the mission of campus ministry throughout your narrative. It was motivational on one hand and provided the how-to (discipleship) on the other. I know all ministers will not have the same experience--but all of us will have struggles and brokenness that relate to other leaders. Our church systems may not be the same, but all of us will face trying times in the midst of whatever style of leadership exists in our church. No matter where we are coming from, I think that your story will help us find grace.

—**Milton Jones**, President of *Christian Relief Fund*

***

With vulnerability and introspection, *Made Competent* is the story of life and ministry. As Casey shares the ups and downs, struggles and joys, lived as a campus minister, husband, and father striving to follow Jesus, we learn about faith, discipleship, and leadership on a mission with God. Such lessons alone warrant reading this book, but I also highly commend this book because I have served in ministry alongside Casey for five years and know that what he writes about is what he lives.

—**K. Rex Butts**, Southside Church of Christ Senior Minister and author of *Gospel Portraits*.

***

Your book is a gift in many ways, but especially to future and current campus ministers. Young ministers, especially, assume that when they encounter a season of difficulty it's their fault, something is wrong with them, they are not really called to this like they thought, etc. Your story beautifully exposes and enlightens such thinking. I think you have a great mix of theology, philosophy, reflection, and anecdotes to encourage a new generation of ministers.

—**Chris Buxton**, ULife Consulting, Inc.

***

This is a book that will help every church leader gain a more caring empathy for what their ministers are experiencing, feeling, and thinking behind their typically gentle, accepting demeanor. There is an increasing scarcity of ministers today, particularly those who have the desire and skill set to lead a church community from the pulpit. When church leaders become frustrated with their minister or lose heart at trying to find someone to fill their preaching role, Casey's book provides deep level insight as to why so few men have the desire to be preachers today and what you can do to create a different trajectory. Thank you, Casey!

—**Stan Granberg**, PhD, *Heritage 21 Foundation*

Made Competent

A Story about Life in Ministry

By
Casey Coston

Published by KHARIS PUBLISHING, an imprint of
KHARIS MEDIA LLC.

Copyright © 2025 Casey Coston

ISBN-13: 978-1-63746-279-9

ISBN-10: 1-63746-279-4

Library of Congress Control Number: 2024950898

Contact the author via caseoncampus@gmail.com

All KHARIS PUBLISHING products are available at special quantity
discounts for bulk purchase for sales promotions, premiums, fund-raising,
and educational needs. For details, contact:

Kharis Media LLC
Tel: 1-630-909-3405
support@kharispublishing.com
www.kharispublishing.com

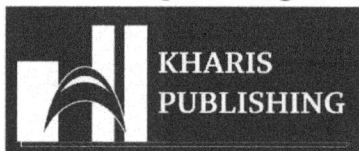

Acknowledgements

There are too many names to honor everyone here so I hope that much of my acknowledgement has already been done in the story itself. Thank you for the role you played in challenging and cheering me on to be made competent. But there are a few groups I simply must honor.

To all the churches I grew up in physically and spiritually, thank you for nurturing my faith until it was my own.

To the North Street Church of Christ (now Mount Comfort) and Scott and Denise Karnes, thank you for investing so much in college students and helping them be Razorbacks for Christ! Go Hogs!

To Mom and Dad, thank you for not discouraging me when I decided to go into ministry. Thank you for trusting me and God. Your support has been so faithful and true. Thank you Rick and Penny for trusting me with your daughter and encouraging me time and time again in my work.

To the Oxford Church of Christ, thank you for walking with me and helping me grow through many dangers, toils and snares. You held me and my family up so many times when life and ministry were painful. To the elders of the church over the entire 15 years, thank you for trusting me to care for students at Ole Miss and loving them to the end.

To the American and International students I cared for at Ole Miss in Rebels for Christ and beyond, please keep following Jesus or considering him until you know enough to make a decision!

To my financial supporters who started with me in Oxford and many who continued on in Delaware, thank you for the faith and trust you have put in me to be a missionary wherever God wants me.

To the Newark Church of Christ, its elders and the Reflect Campus Missions Board, thank you for taking my family in and giving me a second season of ministry to keep growing and loving college students.

To the American and International students at the University of Delaware, I love being a Blue Hen with you. Thank you for your curiosity and courage to consider Jesus and see if he really is who us crazy Christians say he is. I hope you will become a Blue Hen for Christ!

To the major characters in my story, Eric, Milton and Lendy: I would have been lost without your prayers, wisdom and honesty along the way. You are my dearest of spiritual brothers.

Thank you to all my peers and mentors who read my story and helped me tell it better. You were my cloud of witnesses.

Thank you to the entire Kharis Publishing team for believing in my story and helping me share it with the world. I waited and prayed for years and you were God's answer!

To Miles, Maggie and Moses, holding or hugging you has always made the good days better and the hard days more bearable. Love you forever!

To my wounded warrior wife, Tracey, I'm so thankful you let me write out and make some sense of our crazy story in the hope that it can help others who need some comfort and encouragement along life's way. Love you forever and always.

To the next generation of ministers, don't give up and don't lose heart. Keep coming back to Jesus and this book every once-in-a while and may God whisper to you the encouragement you need to go through the painful process of being made competent.

Table of Contents

Introduction

I did not grow up wanting to be a minister, especially a campus minister. I didn't even know that was a profession you could have until I went to college and met my campus minister, Scott Karnes. Now I cannot imagine anything else. Even as I pass 20 years in campus ministry, I hope I can stick around 30 years or more. How did God orchestrate that? What's so great about campus ministry? Why is it, I would argue, one of the best-kept secrets for full-time ministry? I hope my story will take away some of the secrecy. And yet, *any* minister will understand most of my story. Some of the details will be different, but you can still identify the main themes that resonate with your experience. I encourage any minister to listen for those themes. However, this book is not just for current ministers. As you will soon see, it is for anyone who is considering the surprising call of ministry and feels excitement, fear, or both.

There are several reasons why I wanted to write this book. First, I wanted to tell a story. There is something about a story that draws us in and disarms us. I can feel the whole range of human emotions in fiction or nonfiction. Think about this—even a story we *know* is not real (like my favorite: *The Lord of the Rings*) draws us in because there is something even in a fantasy story that resonates with our reality. I also read a few nonfiction books every year. All have good information that is helpful for Bible study and ministry. I will share a few of these throughout my story. Anytime I read one of these ministry books and the author starts telling a story, I read with more interest, I tend to read faster, and it keeps my attention better. Many times, a story is told briefly in a sentence or two and I find myself wanting to know more of the story. I think we humans are divinely wired for this. It's why we read books and watch movies. God created us to be storytellers and story listeners and it's one of the reasons why so much of the Bible is written in story form.

Second, I wanted to tell my story of incompetence and how God made me competent. It is my modest hope that by sharing my failures and my slow but sure growth, any minister will take comfort in knowing that God is at work in us and, often, despite us. For example, it was hard to acknowledge that even with good Bible training, day-to-day ministry made me feel incompetent most of the time—especially in my *first eight years*. Yikes! You will discover for yourself that there are varying levels of pride (the bad kind!), training, and context that affect your competency. Being a first-generation minister also plays a big part. I can see I had lots of chances of giving up and getting out of ministry over the years. But God seemed to provide encouragement and competence at just the right time that kept me in the game. I hope my story will be a tool God uses to keep you in the game.

Third, I firmly believe my incompetence can benefit the larger kingdom of God.

- ANY minister will benefit from reading a ministry story. We have all felt incompetent many times.
- ANY teen, college student, or young adult (i.e. future minister) will benefit from reading a story of what life in ministry could be like. It can encourage you and help you count the cost.
- ANY church leader or member will benefit from reading this story to help them understand and support ministers better.
- ANY minister/spouse will feel the tension of trying to balance family and ministry.
- ANY follower of Jesus can take comfort and courage from how God worked in my incompetence.

Fourth, we need more ministers of all kinds, but I hope you will consider campus ministry. It is no secret that there are fewer ministers available for churches to hire and fewer students going to seminary, but since I'm a campus minister, I will show my bias. Campus ministers are a rare breed and sometimes we can appear to be just older youth ministers or preachers-in-waiting. This book can help educate you and anyone else in some of the uniqueness of our work. I'm praying that a teen, college student, or any young adult will read this and be awakened to the possibility of campus ministry. Currently in my tribe, Churches of Christ, we are on 150-200 campuses and there are over 5,000 campuses (counting community colleges) in the United States. I think there is room for growth, don't you? It will take more first-generation ministers who are willing to go through the painful process of being made competent to reach our lost world and campus. The university mission field is strategic in so many ways, catching young adults at just the right time in their lives seeking answers to life's biggest questions. In a campus community, you enter a whole new world, usually apart from past social bonds, and begin shaping your worldview. "Why am I here?" "What is my purpose?" "How can I provide for myself and be a blessing to others?" "Where does my passion meet the world's pain?" College students are finding their faith which may resemble their parent's faith (though it will not be identical) or they will break with the Christian faith altogether, which sadly, many do. They will also make friends for life and often find a spouse. We need more of you to join us and meet these students at the strategic crossroads of their lives—where faith can help shape the trajectory of their future!

Fifth, I hope you will begin to write your story down. Spoiler alert, I will invite you to reflect on your own experiences and take some time to write down what you remember! *Can you imagine if even 5-10 of us could give the next generation a diverse picture of life in ministry?* And if all you ever do is journal it privately, I assure you it will someday at least be a blessing to your children and grandchildren because it is a time capsule of stories that will help them better understand who you are, where they came from and what you devoted your life to. When I got to the end of one of my journals, I wrote this in April 2015: *"Can't believe I started in January 2004! Thank you for your faithfulness, O Lord! May this especially bless Miles, Maggie, and Moses someday. Love you so much, Daddy."* Now they do not have to become campus ministers, but I want them to see my faith (and my wife's faith in several critical parts of the story) and hear about the good times and tough times I went through because I love Jesus and committed my life to him and how he was faithful time and time again. I hear that fewer and fewer young disciples want to go into ministry due to a variety of perceptions and challenges. I pray that one day, some of them will dream of being a minister again because of something you or I wrote.

Sixth, I needed to experience some healing. As a Christian back in Oxford, Mississippi, taught me through this modern-day proverb: "If you don't heal from what hurt you, you'll bleed on people who didn't cut you." There are a few chapters that were particularly hard to write because of the pain involved. The writing process showed me that I had deceived myself into thinking I was healed or could ignore some places in my heart that still needed healing. Just like a bruise on your skin, you can forget about it until someone touches that spot and then you recoil in pain. I had to write out some of the pain because it had been in my head and heart for years. Nevertheless, now that it is out, I hope to share as one who has been slow to speak, and I earnestly hope to speak the truth in love. It seems so difficult to hold these two together in our culture. Because this story is my limited perspective, I've changed a few names so that I could be honest and still honor those with whom I didn't see eye-to-eye. I hope to be more honest about my weaknesses and failings in the spirit of taking the plank out of my eye first. There are many pressures and anxiety-producing events in these pages. I've learned that while some cope in external ways, I internalize and absorb most of my stress and anxiety. Guess what? That's not good. I'm still learning how to cope with the pressures of marriage, family, and ministry and it is hard work. But I also hope to let go of some baggage.

Finally, before we dive into the story, I want to share with you how to read this book. Where did this "competence" language come from? It came from my favorite book of the Bible: 2 Corinthians. Paul says, *"Not that we are competent in ourselves to claim anything for ourselves, but our competence comes from God. He has made us competent as ministers of a new covenant...."*[1] God is the one who has slowly but surely made me competent. Over time I have allowed him, willingly and reluctantly, to conform my life to the life of Jesus. In the process, I realized that my story is a gospel story, similar in structure to the four gospel accounts in the Bible. I could have molded my book into "Ten Tips for Ministers" with anecdotes along the way, but that book has already been done well.[2] I wanted to write a meditation on ministry that told a twenty-year story of God at work in my incompetence. Over time I learned a lot despite my incompetence because God *knows* we will be incompetent. How could we not be? Does a five-year-old look the same as a twenty-year-old? Of course not. Does a parent know how to parent at the beginning? Hardly. Does God expect someone who has been in ministry for one year to have the same competence, wisdom, and insight as someone who has been serving for twenty years? I hope not. But he gives us more grace and helps us grow.

There's teaching and wisdom here that remind me of the highs and lows that Jesus experienced in his earthly ministry. There are twists and turns, ups and downs, many joys, and my share of sorrows. And by the end, there will be death and resurrection. That's ultimately what makes it a gospel story. No, not a literal death and resurrection but the kind that comes to all students of Jesus if you follow him long enough. If you participate in his life, you will die and be raised daily, monthly, and yearly. Isn't that what we signed up for in our baptism? So thank you for joining me on this journey. The exciting thing is, if you are following Jesus, you too are living a death and resurrection story that is getting played out on God's beautiful kingdom timeline. I pray you

---

[1] 2 Corinthians 3:5-6

[2] Steve Shadrach and Paul Worcester, *The Fuel and the Flame: Ignite your life and your campus for Jesus Christ,* Fayetteville: Center for Mission Mobilization, 2021.

begin to see your life that way and someday tell the world how you were made competent.

Reflect

- *What were some moments where you felt incompetent in your past or feel incompetent now?*

- *Which one of my six reasons for writing stands out to you the most and why?*

Section 1:

The Calling

01

Origin Story

*"We have done so relying not on worldly wisdom
but on God's grace." 2 Corinthians 1:12*

I never dreamed I would be a campus minister—very few do. I wanted to be a weatherman first. I was fascinated by snow and hurricanes. I even imagined being a storm chaser hunting down tornadoes. Anyone who knows my cautious, careful, calculating demeanor and my insurance-selling father will laugh at that. I remember peeking out the window in the night looking to see if the weatherman was right about the snow forecasted for Pine Bluff, Arkansas. He was usually wrong. The disappointment led me to consider being a band director. I loved music. My parents and both sets of grandparents teamed up to buy me a used piano for $800 in 1985. I took lessons for ten years. I still have the piano with me. What an investment! In Junior High, I joined the band and took up the trombone. A few years later, I joined the choir singing baritone. I loved marching and concert bands. I loved choral music and show tunes (though I hope you never see the tapes). God seemed to have given me these gifts and I had a passion for using them. I'm sure my parents would've ultimately been supportive based on how they later reacted to an even crazier idea, but they cautioned me that being a music teacher would be a difficult life: hard on my family and, let's be honest, not pay much. I'm sure they were right. So, I recalibrated again. I was competent at math and science and enjoyed both throughout high school. By my senior year, I was taking physics and calculus. I was getting to use all of my brain, the right side for band and choir and the left side for math and science.

Besides a great academic experience, I was blessed spiritually in the Hazel Street Church of Christ and our modest-sized youth ministry. I was there every time the doors were open. My family's faith was few on words but big on action and participation. I learned to incorporate words more by giving devotionals and helping with the singing. My favorite memories in youth group revolve around going to Youth-in-Action in Jonesboro, Arkansas, to hear great speakers from our tribe like Jeff Walling, Joe Beam, and Don McLaughlin. They always pierced my heart and challenged me to follow Jesus.

My church family encouraged me to consider ministry but with my math and science skills, I chose to focus on engineering. After I visited the University of Arkansas (U of A) on an official visit, I heard that chemical engineers received the highest-paying jobs of any bachelor's degree. I was sold! I was a competent college student, but I didn't love engineering. My life became more about what I could do than what God wanted me to do. I just thought he would want me to do math and science because I was good at it—and that could be true but it's not a guarantee. At a young age, I had not developed a way to discern between worldly and spiritual wisdom. I do know there was some worldly wisdom involved because money was a big reason for my engineering decision. Even a young Christian with loving, Christian parents has mixed motivations. I'm sure there's some "American Dream" motivation in all of us. We would like to live a successful life as defined by our culture, but I'm sure my parents were praying and hopefully I was as well. By my senior year at Arkansas, I recognized that my heart wasn't in engineering and that God was leading me down a path of discernment toward something very different. What on earth could have caused such a huge shift in my choice of career?

Reflect

- *What did you want to be when you were growing up and why?*

- *Who or what was influencing and motivating your decisions in high school and college?*

02

A Second Conversion

"Once more Jesus put his hands on the man's eyes. Then his eyes were opened, his sight was restored, and he saw everything clearly." Mark 8:25

I thought I went to the U of A in 1996 for two main reasons. First, to get a chemical engineering degree so I could start making the big bucks. I even justified it further by saying I would support any of my friends who went on to be missionaries. How noble! Second, to play in the marching band. Go hogs! But as is often the case, I did not take into account how God would work through my campus minister, Scott, and the Razorbacks for Christ (RFC) campus ministry. Scott was certainly a great mentor to me. As time went on, we had more and more conversations about life, love, faith, and my future. Scott loved me well and worked hard to love everyone well. Actually, it didn't seem like he had to work all that hard. God had so captured his heart that he loved us college students with ease. I still hope one day to grow up to be like Scott in that respect. So, campus ministry was not the reason I went to the U of A, but it became the reason my life went in such a different direction. This is often the case with Christian students going to a state school. I can imagine God saying, "Casey thinks he is going to college for engineering and music, but I've got something else in mind for him that he can't even imagine yet."

Slowly but surely, God began to nudge me. In the summer of 1998 before my junior year, I had a wonderful experience in Romania with some fellow RFCs. We spent a month there teaching English using the Bible and developing wonderful relationships with Romanian students our age who were interested in improving their English. We also loved the missionary family. I remember how broken-hearted we were to leave.

Still, I came back focused on a hard junior year of engineering. I began to take on some responsibilities with the campus ministry, caring for fellow students, calling and inviting them to come to an event or Bible study. I was blessed with a solid band of brothers to be stupid and serious with. One of my favorite memories was a group of us guys gathering on the Old Main lawn on Thursday nights to pray. Most of us ended up in ministry for a while. I also tried to date during this time. I had some interest in a few of the women in our ministry, but the timing never seemed right with them. Instead, I dated a sweet Singaporean chemical engineering student for six months who had faith in Jesus but whose faith tradition was different than mine. This was challenging but spiritually formative. Her family was not thrilled that she was dating me and that came as a shock. I thought I was good marriage material, but that made dating difficult because I came on too strong and was committed to the relationship to the bitter end. My heart always wanted to believe she was "the one." We were growing apart in the final month or two; our communication wasn't great because she was gone the spring semester for an internship at Eastman Chemical in Batesville, AR. When it finally came down to the end, I knew she was going to be the one to break up with me because I just couldn't do it. Yes, there was some love, but I confess there was some idolatry too—I had made her too important in my life. She mercifully ended it.

I did a summer internship in 1999 with the same Eastman Chemical. I still remember getting paid $14.25 an hour. They also awarded me a scholarship for my senior year totaling $4000. Combining this with another scholarship that my favorite professor, Dr. Turpin, had recommended me for, the U of A was actually paying me to go to school my senior year. As you can imagine, I went into my final year focused on engineering and feeling blessed beyond belief that God would pave my way so smoothly, taking away so many financial burdens that come with college. In the fall, I remember my dad beginning to talk with me about new cars for graduation. I was driving a 1993 Honda Accord, but I had my eye on a new 2000 Accord. It is telling that I was taking all this good financial news as a sign that God was encouraging me to stay in engineering. That makes sense, right? But that too was worldly wisdom talking. Only later did I look back and see that God was just minimizing my debt for the plans he had in mind.

Even though engineering and music took up a lot of time, I was also pouring myself into the campus ministry. I remember a few students coming to me for spiritual help. We had a guys' Bible study in my dorm. We had a

Tuesday night devotional that included a meal, plus Scott or a student giving a message and lots of time for singing. This occurred in our student center living room which was jam-packed with students. We grew significantly during those years. I know we consistently had 80-90 students coming. I was allowed to share a lesson one Tuesday night which focused on the story of Jesus in the garden. As the prophet Jeremiah or the men on the road to Emmaus described, there was a burning in my heart. There was so much joy and excitement but there was also a pain I was connecting with that I had not experienced before then. I remember one student in particular came up to me after my lesson to say something but quickly left because she was getting emotional. I had never experienced touching a spiritual nerve like that.

Two other things touched a spiritual nerve in me. First, as I was leaving Walmart one night, I noticed the Salvation Army volunteer. As I passed her bucket, I had some change and decided to put it in. I'm not sure I had ever done that before. As I walked to my car, I felt a feeling of joy and pride that I had put my few coins in the bucket. It was brief, however, because in the next few seconds, a deep conviction came over me with words something like, "Really, Casey? You think that is going to solve the world's problems?" It was as close to the voice of God as I had ever heard. It wasn't mean and I didn't feel guilt per se. Conviction is really the best word because within me welled up a deep sense that God was calling me to more than I had previously considered giving. God didn't want my money, he wanted me.

Second, back at home for the Christmas break, my grandma had given me a VHS tape (google it) of *The Visual Bible: Matthew*, a visual, word-for-word depiction of Matthew's Gospel. We've come a long way in twenty-plus years and I highly recommend you watch *The Chosen* now.[3] But this visual representation of Jesus resonated deep within my heart, and I saw the gospel stories come alive. By the time they showed the scenes of Jesus' crucifixion and death, I was a wreck. I wept alone in my home. Again, it wasn't a feeling of guilt. It was a realization of everything Jesus had done for me. Now the thought came—how can I best live my life to honor and thank Jesus for all he did for me?

Notice these encounters were really simple. There were small things God did in my life that made a big impact. He already had my attention, so it didn't take much to get me going in the direction he wanted. All of these experiences contributed to what I have heard described as a *second conversion*. I had already

---

[3] It's a free app: (https://apps.apple.com/us/app/the-chosen/id6443956656)

committed my life to Jesus in baptism when I was 15. This college experience was similar but different. At 15, I was the blind man Jesus touched once and saw people who looked like trees.[4] Now at 22, I had been touched a second time and was seeing the world and people clearly. God had won me over. I knew what I wanted to do: I wanted to go into full-time ministry.

Now I had to tell my parents. I had no idea how they would respond. Even though they are loving, supportive Christian parents, I still had a lot of fear. I knew this would catch them by surprise. Perhaps the hardest part was that I didn't have a plan moving forward, only a conviction that I could not continue down the path of engineering. So, while the world was preparing for Y2K, I was truly walking by faith as I prepared for my unknown future in a new millennium. I don't remember if I shared all these experiences with them or just told them about the conviction, but I sat them down (What child sits his parents down?) and gave them the gist of the story. They listened intently. They did not interrupt me or seem to get angry. I know they saw and heard my conviction. They could see that God was doing something in my heart. They were ultimately supportive of me, praise God! All they asked was that I finish my engineering degree, which I planned to do for no other reason than so I could finish my senior year in the campus ministry. I'm sure they wondered, like I did, what the future would hold.

Next, I told Scott, my home church, my college church, and the RFCs about my big decision. Everyone was encouraging. Ironically, the comment I remember getting the most in response to my big news was, "Well, at least you will have your engineering degree to fall back on if needed." I suppose I could have been wrong about my conviction and how God was at work in my life, but I knew what I felt in my heart and the process through which God had taken me. Cautious, careful, son-of-an-insurance-agent Casey was either crazy or following a call from God. Now, I am very proud of my engineering degree because it was a lot of hard work, I made some great friends, and Dr. Turpin was an amazing professor and follower of Jesus. We need plenty of Jesus-following engineers out there, but I have honestly never once wanted to go back to engineering.[5]

P.S. During the same month as my life-changing decision, I would later learn there was a young woman in West Texas who was also going through a

---

[4] Mark 8:22-26

[5] *"Come, follow me,' Jesus said, 'and I will send you out to fish for people.' At once they left their nets and followed him."* Mark 1:17

major life change breaking off her engagement. I've always wondered if our two separate life-changing events had set us on a course to meet each other.

Reflect

- *What do the signs in your life seem to be pointing to? How might those signs be reframed by the kingdom of God?*

- *How supportive do you think your family would be if you decided to go into full-time ministry?*

- *What calling have you received from God or are sensing currently?*

03

A Divine Nudge

I finished out the spring semester and eventually decided that I would follow in the footsteps of Scott and fellow RFCs by going to Abilene Christian University (ACU) for graduate education. I remember the lonely drive from Fayetteville to the wilderness of West Texas and shed quite a few tears grieving the life I was leaving behind. I only knew three people when I arrived in Abilene. Two of them were RFCs: John and Derrick. These dear brothers of mine kept me sane and gave me something tangible and familiar to hold onto while leaving behind the comforts of all I knew back in Arkansas. The third person was Gwynneth Curtis, a missionary-in-residence, who taught at ACU. He had been integral in the European mission adventures of Scott and had occasionally visited Fayetteville.

On my first Saturday in Abilene…in August…I helped Gwynneth work on a fence in his backyard in 100-degree heat. We talked about the many churches in Abilene—their style, personality, and size. He helped me pick out a church to visit on my first Sunday there. I honestly can't remember which one we had settled on. Why? Later that night, he called me to say he had called a different church, the Baker Heights Church of Christ, and told them I was coming. Wait, what? Talk about the wind blowing in one direction and the Spirit deciding to go a different direction. Three and a half years later, this church had let me work two internships with them when money was tight in between graduation and leaving Abilene.

Soon after joining Baker Heights, I met and began a friendship with Tracey Laing. Her long, blond hair was stunning. She had a great sense of humor, but I could see some sadness in her eyes. For the first year, I wisely focused on friendship since she was coming out of a rough relationship and broken engagement. I actually wrote her a farewell letter at the end of the first year because it seemed she would be moving to a new job in a new city. But that summer, she stayed put and we started emailing a lot. By the time I returned for year two, I had gotten up the courage to ask her for a date. She had already graduated and was working for the local newspaper as a photojournalist. She had to go in early on September 11th and look at all the devastating pictures that were coming in off the Associated Press (AP) wire. When she got off work that night, we went to IHOP to process everything. We went to IHOP again on the 16th and started dating. Nine months later we were married on June 8th, 2002. However, just before the wedding, Tracey was in the hospital for several days. The stress of wedding preparations had actually caused her immune system to flare. She was diagnosed with a rare auto-immune disease. (I tried not to take it personally!) There was talk of getting married in the hospital but thankfully lots of steroids got her on the right track for the short term. If ever there was a count-the-cost marriage moment, this was it, but I was undeterred! The course of my life had changed forever, and I owed it all to Gwynneth and God's divine nudge.

Reflect

- *When did God do something mysterious to change the course of your life?*

04

Equipped...Kind of.

"He has made us competent as ministers..." 2 Corinthians 3:6

So let's start with the good news. I absolutely loved my time at ACU.[6] In my first semester, fall of 2000, I took Dr. David Wray's *Spiritual Formation* class, and it changed my life. One of our assignments was to write a spiritual autobiography. I had never even thought of writing down my story. It was healing for me to write it and for Dr. Wray to read it and affirm my spiritual journey. He appreciated the journey that had led me to ACU. I was also his Graduate Assistant, and we developed a great friendship. He made himself available to me even when he was very busy. I confess this is something I was slow to learn as a minister.

I loved so many of my classes and professors. I enjoyed learning Greek and Hebrew but could listen all day to Dr. Osburn tell his translation stories and how Greek helped with real life issues, like marriage and divorce. I loved discovering things I had never noticed before in *Introduction to the New Testament* and *New Testament Theology*. I'll never forget the police ride-along I did for Dr. Wray's class when I shook hands (when I wasn't supposed to) with a lady who had supposedly been on the Jerry Springer show. I appreciated the history, language, theology, and practical ministry dimensions of my degree program in every way.

---

[6] Financially, I got some good academic scholarships, and I interned for churches most summers to help pay for school.

But by the time I graduated in December 2003 and was looking for jobs, I seemed to have forgotten something important. As I searched for ministry opportunities, I looked for preaching positions, youth ministry, and a variety of others. These were the pathways ACU offered to get you into full-time ministry. Do you see my problem? These three and a half wonderful years had unintentionally caused me to forget what had sent me there in the first place—campus ministry. I honestly doubt there was one word devoted to contextualizing what I had learned at ACU for public university campus ministry.[7] I was equipped so well to be a minister and I could certainly argue that I was equipped theologically to do any kind of ministry. God was beginning to make me competent, but for campus ministry? No.[8] Now it's certainly true that even if campus ministry changes your life, that doesn't mean you have to go into full-time campus ministry, but I was beginning to think that's what God had in mind for me.

Reflect

- *How well did your Christian education prepare you for ministry?*

- *What gaps were there in your training?*

---

[7] For example, in hindsight, I would recommend that a practical course like domestic missions or church planting or church growth incorporate some awareness of the campus mission field and the need to plant new campus ministries.

[8] There have been some welcome changes to this that I will talk about later in my chapter "Closing the Loop." But if you need to know more now, read that chapter and contact my campus minister friend, Chris Buxton, and tell him I sent you. chris@ulifeconsulting.org

05

Why Not Youth Ministry?

Iinterviewed for a preaching position or two with no success. It was good interview practice, but the hot-button questions asked by search committees and elders were hard for me to address coming out of grad school. I started taking a youth ministry position in Phoenix, Arizona, seriously because some dear friends of mine from the campus ministry at Arkansas were there: Matt and Amber. Matt and I had gone to Romania and sang in choir together, and he had been a year ahead of me in chemical engineering. It was exciting to be traveling and interviewing for jobs, but this youth ministry position unsettled me. Here is what I wrote in my journal after returning from the interview:

> **January 14, 2004:** *"George (one of the elders) called last night, and they want to ask some more questions next Monday night. With that phone call, the confidence and security I had with the Phoenix job suddenly disappeared. I knew I could fall back on that job if I needed to. That is obviously not the way to approach a job, but it is easy to do. Now I find myself helpless again, having nowhere to firmly stand. I wonder what questions they will ask.... Maybe they will want to ask me about my passion and commitment to youth ministry. I still don't know how to answer that."*

Honestly, I did not see myself as a youth minister. Perhaps I was basing it off years of VBS and knowing how hard it was for me to be the fun, cool guy leading anyone younger than 18 years old. It took me all of my twenties to realize I wasn't going to be the fun, cool guy for any age group. Certainly, the meeting with parents in Phoenix was beginning to tip me off to the complications of working not only with young people but also their parents. I could hear the history of past issues in their questions that I was oblivious too. I was also naïve enough to think I could come in as the new guy and fix them. Thankfully, I was willing to discern with some trusted advisors, so I reached out to Robert Olgesby, Jr., a professor of youth ministry at ACU. Here's that journal entry:

January 21, 2004: *"In talking with Robert, I explained my struggle with Phoenix and youth ministry. He talked a lot in terms of ministry that either drains or energizes you. All ministry can be draining, but I sensed him saying that even when you're physically drained, your passion for that ministry helps you overcome whatever draining occurs. And even if you're drained, it is not resented or unexpected because this is the kind of ministry worth doing. Somewhere in the midst of that is the energy to endure, a joy in the journey. He said he could see me doing campus ministry because there is some consistency with pulpit preaching. He also warned that the parents do present a dynamic not present in campus ministry."*

It is significant that Robert emphasized campus ministry. When he said that, it was like a light bulb went off in my mind. Of course, campus ministry—the thing I had forgotten about for three and a half years. I could see myself enduring in campus ministry. Given my natural tendency to avoid conflict and not having a good skill set in that area, youth ministry began to fade. As I said with engineers, I say again with youth ministers: we need them. I worked with some dear brothers who poured their lives into teenagers. I saw their passion for that age group and could tell they were where God wanted them. I just discerned that youth ministry was not for me. It did not fit my skill set, personality, and spiritual gifts. But the important thing was that I had reached out to my spiritual community to help me make a wise decision. Thus, God protected me from a false start and almost certainly a short stint as a youth minister.

Reflect

- *Who do you go to for clarity in times of uncertainty?*

- *How confident are you in your particular ministry of choice right now? What gives you that confidence?*

06

The Road to Ole Miss

"Do I make my plans in a worldly manner…?" 2 Corinthians 1:17

I don't recall thinking much about Ole Miss growing up even though they were just one state over from me. I do remember the seven-overtime thriller in 2003 when the Arkansas football team beat Eli Manning and Company in Oxford. And with that statement, I've just alienated all my Rebel friends. Sorry/not sorry!

The first time Ole Miss made it into my journal was in January 2004. They were part of a short list of ministry opportunities I was considering. In February I wrote this: *"Called Scott (my campus minister) on Tuesday…he did call his friend in Oxford and talked me up. The search committee emailed the next day to set up a phone interview for Thursday night. We had a really good conversation that night and ever since then, I have felt very strongly about this ministry. I feel like I want to go there so much, and it seems like the perfect job for me for a long time. I hope and pray that this is where we will go and yet—thy will be done."*

The phone interview went well, and I learned we would visit Oxford in March. I was excited but anxious. In late February I wrote: *"We go to Oxford next weekend for a big interview and I have such good feelings about it and yet I simply must say, 'Thy will be done.' In an important decision like this that will affect so many souls, I know God has a keen interest in this and may very well want this for us. But he could obviously know something I don't. I keep thinking that 'thy will be done' would bring a sense of peace into my heart. But that is not the case."*

We had a great visit. It was spring break so there were only a few grad students in town. We met with all the elders and interested church members.

Apparently, the interview went well because afterward, I wrote this on **March 15**[th]: *"What a wonderful time to be living! Praise be to the God who works all things for good, who accomplishes his will in his perfect time. As I write on this Sunday, I have a job, a ministry, a place to serve my great God, and it is such a great place to start and maybe even stay in ministry. The Oxford Church of Christ in Oxford, Mississippi, is our destination, and 'campus minister' is God's calling to me. First, we met Bob and Linda in Texarkana and visited for about two hours at the IHOP. Bob had just been hired as the new pulpit preacher. As we continued driving back to Abilene, we were approaching Dallas around 5:30 pm when we got a call from Eric (one of the elders). He called to say Bob had confirmed the elder's impression of us and based on that, they were ready to offer me the job."*

Eric went through the details of the very generous offer. In my journal I continued: *"Well, I was overwhelmed and told Eric that all our big questions had been answered and that we were prepared to accept the offer now. He immediately started waxing poetically about God calling us to Oxford (this is something Eric was good at and would do often over the years), praising God for this new relationship, saying he would make a gleeful announcement Sunday morning and that he was on his knees in prayer thanking God. Just this information alone says a lot about Eric as a spiritual man. Tracey had been so impressed with our wrap-up meeting because we gathered in a circle, held hands, and the elders all got on one knee. If I could think of one thing about the weekend interview to remember now, it is the elders. They prayed every time we were together, asked good, appropriate questions, and did everything to help us, especially Tracey. They are diverse but loving, unified but different. I praise God for these elders!"*

I share all of this for several reasons. First, campus ministries in Churches of Christ are normally under the umbrella of a local church and its elder leadership. The elders function as shepherds of the local body and all its ministries. They provide guidance and protection because of their collective wisdom.[9] Second, it is important to celebrate the joyful moments when God acts in such a clear and beautiful way. This was vindication of the decision I had made by faith *over four years earlier* to go into ministry. Third, it is important to remember these moments because sometimes God's work in our lives is not so clear when hardships come our way. Part of our endurance comes from remembering those times when God has clearly worked. This was always the function of the exodus and the empty tomb. Finally, it is important

---

[9] This is a dynamic that some of you are familiar with while others of you have more experience with a regional board or simply reporting to a more experienced staff member on your team. The important thing is that someone probably functions like an elder in your life.

to remember that God is always using the body of Christ to carry out his purposes for the world. Scott, the search committee, and the eldership were part of his body that he used to bring Tracey and I to Ole Miss. I remember that time with great fondness. That first-job feeling was so pure and hopeful after living in the wilderness of West Texas for a season. It must have felt something like that time Jesus left the wilderness and headed for Galilee.

Reflect

- *What was it like when you were hired for your first full-time ministry position?*

- *If you are still preparing for your first full-time position, write about an internship you got or hope to get.*

Section 2:

The Incompetent Years

07

Afraid of Evangelism

"I will not boast about myself, except about
my weaknesses." 2 Corinthians 12:5

We got settled into Oxford in April 2004 and finished out the semester. The church welcomed us with open arms. The current students seemed happy to have me. The interim campus minister, Benny, an African American man, took me under his wing for a few months showing me the ropes. He had some health issues but was a jolly fellow with a great smile and infectious laugh. I will never forget the way he would introduce me to nearly everyone: "This is the man who took my job." The first time was a little awkward, but after that it became funny. You just had to know Benny.

I had the joy of attending my first campus ministry conference in Morgantown, West Virginia, in late July.[10] Jason Locke was the hosting campus minister. I had actually met him through Scott years earlier. It was cool to be in a beautiful college town. It was even cooler to be part of a conference that was devoted to campus ministry.

I wrote down lots of sound bites at the conference in my notebook. One in particular stood out to me that I have used for years. It was shared by Dr. Evertt Huffard, Dean of Harding School of Theology (HST): *"We will never evangelize people we fear or hate."* I knew he was thinking of our Muslim neighbors and students since we were still recovering from 9/11 and he had grown up

---

[10] Check out what is now the Campus for Christ conference at campusforchrist.org

in Israel, but these words haunted me. I wasn't afraid of certain kinds of people. God had taught me to love all kinds. I was just afraid of evangelism PERIOD. It felt like the scariest word in the Christian dictionary to a scaredy cat like me. I know that sounds strange for someone going into campus ministry whose job is to reach all kinds of students, but I was afraid of sharing my faith with anyone who wasn't already a Christian and I didn't see a practical way to overcome my fear. This made my early years at Ole Miss difficult, to say the least. It was easy to meet Christians in the saturated South, but I had so many questions:

- How do you find seekers and skeptics?
- How do you start conversations with them and keep the conversation going?
- How do you balance your time between the 99 and the one? (See Luke 15)
- How do you deal with rejection and awkwardness?
- Why am I afraid? What's the worst that can happen?
- Are there other ways of doing evangelism?
- Is love enough to reach new people? Is it stronger than fear?

So many questions and very few answers.

The conference ended with the vision Jason cast for the Northeast. These words were included in the notebook:

"We believe that a new burst of campus ministry and church planting is on the horizon. Our churches are establishing programs in Pittsburgh, Buffalo, and at the University of Delaware. Other new and innovative church plants exist in New York City and beyond. We sense that the Lord is offering us an open door for work among university students and young people."[11]

There was hope but it didn't help my timidity that there were Christians out there who had abused evangelism.[12] Was I capable of that? I think we all are. Paul tells us this about the Corinthians and some of their favorite leaders: "In fact, you even put up with anyone who enslaves you or exploits you or takes advantage of you or puts on airs or slaps you in the face."[13] I remember Jason sharing a video showing the states, universities, and their enrollments

---

[11] Jason Locke, National Campus Ministry Seminar Conference Notebook, 2004.
[12] Thomas A. Jones, *In Search of a City*, City: Dpi, 2007 gives us a history of some of the blessings and abuses of the Boston Movement.
[13] 2 Corinthians 11:20

in the Northeast that did not have a campus ministry. He invited us to come forward and pray about this mission field, which I did. In many ways, it seemed like an irrelevant end to a wonderful experience as a rookie campus minister who had come just looking for tips and tools that would help me prepare for my first fall in Oxford. All I can say for now is—be careful what you pray for.

Reflect

- *Are you afraid of evangelism, certain groups of people, or both? Why? If you're not afraid, why do you think that is?*

08

The Blessings and Curses of a Building

"The God who made the world…
does not live in temples built by human hands." Acts 17:24

Every minister and church leader has to wrestle with *where* to meet for worship, Bible study, and fellowship. So let me give you a little geography and history. Our church building was at the heart of downtown Oxford but not far from campus and over the years, many students came there on Sunday morning. Doug Shields Sr. was the primary visionary who gathered support to strategically purchase some land for a student center right across from campus. Since 1960, the University Christian Student Center (UCSC) has existed in some form with a few additions over the years. The vision was initially focused on housing Christians who went to school at Ole Miss but were also able to get some Bible credit thanks to a partnership with Harding School of Theology (HST) in Memphis. This was the "Bible Chair" model that occurred in a few other places.[14] During my time, there was a separate men's dorm area in the back, and the main building could house a few women upstairs while the first floor was where most of the ministry was done. Thankfully, the facility and maintenance issues were taken

---

[14] Rick Rowland, *Campus Ministries: A Historical Study of Churches of Christ Campus Ministries and Selected College Ministries from 1706-1990*, Fort Worth: Star Bible Publications, 1991.

Casey Coston

care of by the Student Center Manager.[15] This freed me up to focus on the
mission to students and the campus. I was, in fact, the first campus minister
with Rebels for Christ (RFC) who didn't also have that job. I likely would
have naïvely taken the job either way, but it would have almost certainly
burned me out sooner or split my focus so much that every day would have
been a frustration. I commend the elders for listening to wise counsel and
creating two positions.

The UCSC functioned first as a training ground for disciples to grow in
their faith and then as a haven, or home-away-from-home, for students.
Christian parents had some fears sending their kids to a state school, so
having a strong Christian organization and facility was a comfort to them.
This was another model for our student centers. It was a blessing in many
ways. The parents often told stories about their fond memories. Certainly,
remembering those good times is fine as long as we understand it is not a
guarantee of similar results in the future. There are too many variables that
change over time. In fact, I heard a former campus minister friend give this
wise warning: "The good ol' days only move us to nostalgia, not participation
with the living God." We can be grateful for the past but let us not get stuck
there. We must remember that God, though unchanging in his nature and
character, is constantly adapting to try and reach the world that he loves.

Now if you have worked in a ministry where you have a building, you
understand the blessings and curses that come with it. One obvious blessing
is it is your space to use as you wish, any time you want. One curse is the
constant maintenance and money required for it. I have often heard
parachurch ministries lament the struggle to find space on or near campus to
host their meetings; even when you do find it, you have to jump through the
university's hoops to reserve the space.[16] I want you to know I am pro-
building, but mine was handed to me after years of investment and sacrifice
by those disciples who came before me. I was standing on their shoulders.
There were plenty of times I actually saw the benefit of parachurch groups
like CRU or InterVarsity which had meetings on campus. It seemed more
incarnational to be there among the buildings where students naturally were
every day. It seemed like a harder sell, especially as the years went on, to try

---

[15] I must give a big "thank you" to Melanie Dahl and then Deborah Bone for taking on this
role.
[16] Parachurch groups often don't have one local church sponsoring their work like we did, and
their staff usually raise 100% of their financial support.

and ask students to walk or drive to the Student Center, especially the non-Christian seekers I became more and more interested in reaching.

Even if you are "pro-building," every Christian leader should know the strengths and weaknesses of their position. For example, similar to church buildings, one downside of a facility is that it can function more like an exclusive gym for "members only" instead of a coffee shop where you would invite anyone. It can start so innocently because we experience God's presence there in a special way. Over time, we can forget that God does not live there, as Paul reminds us in Acts 17, but simply continues to meet us there as we invite him into our lives. God could just as easily meet us anywhere else on campus or in the community.[17] Dr. Mark Love's *Evangelism* course at ACU taught me to view our buildings as an outpost. It was a gathering place to come back to and celebrate the work that had been done on campus that day or week. The Memphis Campus Minister, Tim Stafford, had early on talked about viewing our buildings as a third space. Our homes or dorms are the first space and our offices and classrooms as the second space. If the UCSC was to become a third space, it would need to become a welcoming place not just for Christians, but for anyone to come and hang out, study, or discuss the Christian faith. In other words, a place for seekers and skeptics, International and American students. Otherwise, you are left with a few isolated Christians cliquishly hiding out in their safe space away from the scary public university. Even as naturally timid as I was, I knew I did not want that. Over the years, we experienced both the gym and coffee shop mindsets. There were seasons when our group was great at inviting their friends to hang out or join a Bible study. There were seasons when we turned inward, and I had to discern ways to help our students see beyond themselves to the campus God was calling us to love.

Reflect

- *What is the history of your ministry space?*

- *What are the strengths and weaknesses you see with your facility or lack thereof?*

- *If you are a student in training, what do you imagine wanting and why?*

---

[17] The fact that God abandoned the temples built for him by Solomon and Zerubbabel should be a stark warning for us.

09

My First International Student

"Unlike so many, we do not peddle the word of God for profit. On the contrary, in Christ we speak before God with sincerity, as those sent from God."
2 Corinthians 2:17

Church leaders Doug Shields Jr. and Jim Hendrix had invested in international students who came to Ole Miss long before I ever got there. I remember meeting with Jim from time to time. At least one time he showed me picture after picture of international students that he had studied with over the years. Many of them had become Christians while in Oxford. Doug faithfully taught a Sunday morning Bible class for international students that were mostly Chinese friends. I occasionally taught the class over the years, and it was always an exciting challenge to share a Bible lesson with them. Doug emphasized simplifying the message because English was not their primary language and because biblical themes like salvation, grace, and resurrection are hard enough to grasp even when you are a native speaker.

Doug recruited church members who were willing to meet weekly for an hour with an international student. These students were willing to read the Bible to improve their English. Doug made it clear that we used the Bible for the English conversations and most international students were ok with this. We used the Let's Start Talking (LST) workbooks, which use a simpler English translation for beginners. LST calls the ministry "Friend Speak" here in the United States. It must have been Doug who paired me with David, a

Chinese PhD student.[18] We met for the first time in March 2005 when I journaled this: "*Had my first reading session with David today. Who knows how long we will study, how deep our friendship might become, and maybe someday I can call him 'brother.'*" I knew I was making a commitment—every week for an hour. I remember early on thinking, "It's going to be hard to carry on a conversation for an hour," but as the relationship deepened, it got easier. I didn't know how long we would study but I did have this hope that one day, he would be my brother in Jesus. That vision kept me going and you're accomplishing some English work. That is a great service to them, but I knew I didn't just want to improve David's English. I wanted the word of God to do its job and get planted in his heart and grow so that there would be fruit. I think Jesus had a parable about that. Someday I wanted to experience directly or indirectly that David had committed his life to Jesus. Over a year later, we were still meeting when I wrote this on **April 3, 2006**: "*My friend David continues to progress. It does seem like the seed is beginning to grow in him. He talks about the stories with good understanding and he talks about Jesus as if he knows Jesus. He asked me a profound question about the Word—he asked if the Christian life was hard. He noticed that Jesus' life was hard and painful and wondered if his life would be too. I mentioned that the Christian life is both harder and easier. It is harder because of what God calls us to and the suffering we may experience for following Jesus. But it is much easier than living our lives apart from him. It is easier because there is love and joy and peace and the presence and power of God. It is harder because daily we must choose to carry a cross. Thank you for David, God!*"

Honestly, it can take a year to feel like you are making any spiritual progress and getting beyond English comprehension. But the fact is, we had been meeting most weeks for a year and the Word was beginning to do its job. Everyone who has ever studied with an international student or someone who hasn't heard the gospel before knows that they ask the best questions. My heart still hurts when I read those lines about David wrestling with the pain and suffering in Jesus' life and wondering whether the same would be asked of him. I hope you feel that too. As followers of Jesus, we can wince when we truly acknowledge what Jesus went through for us, knowing that some kind of suffering will find us too. This heartburn I felt was similar to the pain I had had in my heart when I gave that devotional in Arkansas years ago. It hurt for sure, but it also felt like I was exactly where I needed to be—

---

[18] Our Chinese friends often take an American name, so it is easier for us to remember and identify them.

investing in David's life and slowly but surely letting the gospel work on his heart. I was witnessing the transformation that was occurring in his life and it felt so sacred and fulfilling.

Some personal events came up soon after this journal entry that prevented me from continuing with David and then David had to go back to China, but I had planted and watered and would learn to trust God to make it grow. David has not become a Christian yet, but I've prayed for him in the writing of this chapter and hope that someday I will get to see him again, no later than eternity, as my brother in Christ.

Reflect

- *What international students/neighbors have you met, befriended, or invested in?*

- *What is the next step you can take with any current international friend?*

10

Coffee House Theology

"But thanks be to God, who…uses us to spread the aroma of the knowledge of him everywhere." 2 Corinthians 2:14

I spent over a year trying to do what a good missionary should do first:
- Listen to the voices that had been there longer than me,
- Look for strengths to build on and weaknesses that might match my strengths,
- Learn the culture of the church, campus ministry, and Ole Miss campus.

As 2006 dawned, God seemed to be moving us toward a new vision for the Student Center that would further bless our work with students. I learned through some research that the best and most effective campus ministries were next to campus and integrated with the church. In other words, we needed to be close to campus and have a healthy partnership with our church family. But this meant we would have to work harder to encourage the church to participate in the campus ministry. This made the most sense theologically as well. Again, Tim in Memphis had taught us, "We have to give up the notion that students must come to us. The church must come to students." I cannot stress enough the natural tendency in our churches to believe the opposite of this—that outsiders or students must come to us. Maybe it came from the revival days when we invited our friends and neighbors to our church buildings, hoping they would come to follow Jesus, but those days are mostly gone in my opinion. There was a hidden resistance in their hearts that took time to overcome and expecting them to show up on Sunday at a strange building with a bunch of strange new people was a tall order. We have to be diligent in reminding the church that God has sent us into the world and thus, to the campus. Looking back, I wish I had spent more time fleshing out the implications of leaving the 99 to go find the one lost sheep because this sums up campus ministry so well. But how does that play out practically? I couldn't just abandon the mostly Christian students who came regularly and yet there were so many lost students.

I learned that even Christian students were hard to involve because a good number of them came to Ole Miss to take a break from their faith. The Solomon effect of applying their minds to study and exploring all that is done under the heavens coincides well with college life.[19] The studious poured into their classes, the social invested in Greek life, and the sports enthusiasts devoted a whole Saturday or more to tailgating and games. It was daunting to see how I could have any effect on these allegiances. Now we were blessed with some amazing Jesus-following students that you will read about, but I know that many Christian students coming to Ole Miss did want to hide their faith and explore college life apart from God at least for a season.

So, I crafted a new vision for the Student Center:

1. New purpose: To be an intersection for the seeker and the saved, a marketplace for the lost and Christian student, a center for all who would come.
2. New function: To be a resource and outpost for mission to campus.
3. New name: The Alpha Omega (AΩ) Christian Student Center

Some of this should sound familiar because of what I said about the Student Center earlier. The name change was my attempt to engage the Greek culture at Ole Miss which was very strong. Sorority Row was right by the Student Center. Greek letters were on their huge pristine houses and cool, colorful t-shirts. I certainly didn't plan on assimilating the ministry into some kind of fraternity or sorority house (if, for no other reason than I had no experience in Greek life). *But I did want to draw attention to the fact that followers of Jesus have Greek letters too.* My only hope was to point students to Jesus who is the Alpha and the Omega, the beginning and the end of everything.

The new vision also included a centerpiece for the mission to campus— a coffee house. We had taken our cue from the Memphis ministry which also had one. We believed the coffee house had many advantages:

---

[19] Ecclesiastes 1:13

- The coffee house would create an environment for the gospel to be shared and heard.
- If the gospel was shared and heard, it created an environment for the mission of God.
- It could become students' "third place" and help protect our building against the exclusive gym mentality.
- Student leaders could be trained in the arts of coffee and building relationships.

We had a generous couple in our church family who kickstarted the fundraising for us. Since I was not a businessman and we couldn't afford to pay a manager and staff full time, we decided to simply take donations for our drinks. We budgeted for the coffee and staffing a few hours a week ($2000 annually). The recipients of the proceeds varied from year to year. We raised $1500-2000 most years for about ten years before the coffee house began to die out.

There were disadvantages:

- It was a struggle to get seeker students into a known Christian building.
- We only used the coffee house around our regular events due to the cost of keeping it open more.
- There was plenty of coffee house competition on and off campus and students often felt more comfortable there.
- We needed a manager besides me who could devote the time needed to make it great. I should have delegated this from the beginning.
- I still didn't know how to facilitate spiritual conversations and train others to do the same.

The coffee house was a big first step for me into attraction ministry. I learned if you are going to do attraction ministry, you really have to go big to get students' attention.[20] I wasn't really gifted or trained for that, and I doubt we had the budget either. We wanted the coffee house to attract students to us, but I was running into the same issue as our church. We were asking students to take a big step of faith coming into our strange building...too big. Besides, it's not the impulse of the incarnation. Jesus left heaven and came to

---

[20] Check out https://wellcoffeehouse.com/ and https://robtouchstone.com/introducing-the-well/ for more info on having a great coffee house.

us, and we must always wrestle with how best to go meet our context where they are. Our little coffee house was a blessing, but I wonder what other ways we could have engaged our campus more effectively.

Reflect

- *What do you see as strengths and weaknesses of the vision and coffee house?*

- *How important do you think it is to have an attraction ministry and why?*

- *What are some ideas you think would be a good way to reach students today?*

11

Church Politics 101—
Participant

"Therefore, be as shrewd as snakes and as innocent as doves." Matthew 10:16

Let's break down the phrase "church politics." It's one of those things we wish didn't happen or think shouldn't happen in the body of Christ. It's also one of those things I know when I see it but it's a little hard to define. Let me try:

- First, church politics is trying to take into account the thoughts and feelings of everyone involved in a situation that is complex and has the potential for conflict.

- Second, the goal of our politicking is to minimize conflict if at all possible and reach a healthy and peaceful solution.

- Third, as Jesus taught his disciples, be innocent as doves but as shrewd as serpents in the process. As you can imagine, being innocent and shrewd is a tricky combination to pull off, and the disciples of Jesus struggle to do it well. Innocence without shrewdness is naivety. Shrewdness without innocence is manipulation. Most of us tend to be naturally one or the other and have to learn with the Spirit's help how to have a balance.

A situation arose early in my ministry that would put our church leadership to the test. I did not play a big role, though I was a participant. The Student Center and campus ministry had for a long time been run by a Board of Directors—meaning alumni whose lives had been impacted by the Student Center and wanted to see it continue to flourish for future generations. But the Board's involvement had slowly declined over the years and it seemed like a good time to consider a transition to elder oversight by the Oxford Church of Christ. Here is my account of the special board meeting.

February 2006: *"Yesterday was a momentous and historic day. The morning had started hopeful when we learned that one long-standing board member had resigned. He would not be coming and thus, not affecting the day's events. Later during the meeting, we found out that 2-3 more members had resigned over the weekend. These were the precise members we had worried about and planned contingency plans for if they caused a stink. And though these brothers had resigned, Doug Jr. comforted us by saying that these brothers disagreed with our new direction but had said it in a Christian manner. Truly it should be okay for people to disagree! But with the Board members currently present, President Lin Garner asked me to present my proposal. Everyone had already read it, but I felt it important to connect them to the vision and to me who they barely knew. I finished my presentation and members proceeded to ask a few general questions. People were in general agreement with the idea and supportive. Finally, Doug Sr. (one of the visionaries for the campus ministry) had the floor and began to make the day more historic. He proceeded to tell the history of the UCSC since 1960. As he moved towards his plea, he raised his arms almost in praise and jubilation to say that we had a campus minister and elders who had a dream. He concluded with a motion to transfer ownership of the property to the Oxford Church of Christ. After some healthy discussion, a vote was called for. Lin asked for those in favor and a chorus of 'aye's' rang out. When the call for those opposed was made, there was the sweet sound of silence. Several had expressed their pleasure that the campus ministry and Student Center were now under the oversight of the local church and its elders, saying they wished it could have been this way from the beginning. Afterward, the conversations looked and sounded like those of saints who were content, at peace, excited about how the day had gone, and how hopeful the future in Christ looked for the campus ministry. Truly, all I could really say was, 'The battle did belong to the Lord.' No one else could have made such a huge decision happen so quickly, unanimously, and peacefully. To God be the glory!"*

Here you can see there was a delicate tension between the campus ministry Board and the local elders. We tried to handle the transfer of power as best we could, and I believe God blessed it. I am not a big fan of tension and conflict. Who is, right? This particular issue was resolved peacefully. The Board was dying, and the elders were willing to take on oversight. I've learned over the years, however, that some tensions never fully disappear. There is always a tension between church and campus, family and ministry, evangelism and discipleship. You will have some similar and unique tensions based on your context. But I'm getting ahead of myself. We will talk more about these tensions later. For now, we had our vision, facilities, and leadership personnel in place to prepare for an exciting future of missions at Ole Miss. There was just one problem—something was just around the corner that no one could prepare for.

Reflect

- *What are some church politics you have heard stories about or experienced firsthand?*

- *What are some tensions in your life that are not easily resolved?*

- *What is your relationship with conflict?*

12

The Great Sadness

"We were under great pressure, far beyond our ability to endure, so that we despaired of life itself. Indeed, we felt we had received the sentence of death."
2 Corinthians 1:8-9

I did not read *The Shack* until 2010 but something traumatic happens in the book called "The Great Sadness." It seems that most everyone experiences a great sadness at some point in their lives and I couldn't think of a better title for what follows.

In April 2006, Tracey was pregnant with our first child, Miles. After a week of unusual abdominal pain (and moving her to a Memphis hospital), the medical staff took her back for a C-section on April 13th (six weeks before her due date). I sat alone in the assigned "new dad" chair waiting to be called back. They ushered me into the surgery room. I went over to Tracey—she was thankful to be feeling no pain for the first time in a week. I stroked her head and held her hand. I felt so much love for her. The nurses told us when Miles was out at 6:31 pm. He let out a good cry and we knew that was a good thing. Miles was little but healthy. We both started crying as we felt a sense of relief, peace, and joy. But then we heard the word "quandary." There was a film on Tracey's organs and an odor and things no one had seen before. We heard the word "hysterectomy" and immediately got scared, but thankfully that was not done. To make a long story short, we discovered that the annoying little organ called the appendix had ruptured sometime recently, causing all her pain and the early birth. And for that, Tracey's body would pay a terrible price.

A general surgeon would soon have to perform a procedure to remove an abscess the size of a football from her abdomen. The infection was terribly widespread. Tracey's incision from the C-section got infected and started oozing out. When the doctor and nurses came in to clean it up, Tracey said it was the most pain she'd ever felt.

On May 1, Tracey got to go home. It was the 26th day since she had first entered the hospital. She was frail, but we thought the worst was over. Thankfully during this time, the elders gave me a letter addressing our unique situation. My compensation would continue uninterrupted, and they gave me this encouragement:

"The elders sincerely appreciate your efforts to guide your ministry under these very challenging circumstances. Please know that the elders and church family are in constant prayer for Tracey and Miles. May God work in a very special way to bring about complete recovery for Tracey."

It was already at the bottom of my list of concerns, but I was so thankful for this grace so that I could continue to focus on my wife and NOT worry about my job. The paychecks would keep coming though I was giving practically nothing to ministry work at the time. When you believe in good and evil, you know that things like this can feel evil. It felt like Tracey had stepped on a medical landmine with terrible consequences. Maybe it was just a natural evil because our bodies do fail us from time to time, but it's possible that Satan took an interest in our situation because he saw the potential for good in our family and at Ole Miss and knew that he had to intervene. Like Paul said in 2 Corinthians 2:11, "We are not unaware of his schemes." To know that Satan is scheming against the people and mission of God is unnerving. We can't always outmaneuver him because we can't always see what's coming. Perhaps even more unnerving is that God allows this suffering. Whatever it was, it felt like Paul's "sentence of death." Prayer was the main way we fought against the devil's schemes. As you will see, the need for prayer was just beginning.

P.S. From my journal dated 5/5/2010—four years later.

"I thought recently about all that time I spent in the hospital with Tracey and how the elders permitted me to stay with her as long as needed. I thought about how God did that to protect me from dangerous forms of escape if I had been at home with Miles by myself at night. I could have been destroyed. But our marriage is strong, and Satan was thwarted from his schemes. May his schemes continue to be thwarted by the Spirit's power!"

Resource: Bessel Van Der Kolk in *The Body Keeps the Score*, will help you understand your trauma better and offer some treatment possibilities.

13

The Long Sadness

"But we have this treasure in jars of clay to show that this all-surpassing power is from God and not from us." 2 Corinthians 4:7

"I was sure by now that you would have reached down and wiped our tears away, stepped in, and saved the day. But once again, I say 'Amen' and it's still raining." Casting Crowns, "Praise You in This Storm"

It would have been wonderful if Tracey had simply and slowly healed. Unfortunately, our great sadness would turn into a long sadness. I'm giving you this much detail for two reasons. First, we identified with Paul's experience in 2 Corinthians—great pressure, far beyond our ability to endure, and the sentence of death. Tracey's tremendous bodily and emotional trauma and mine secondhand, forced us to rely on God, who raises the dead. Second, these events would *forever* change my professional life as a campus minister. *You will only understand some of the things still to come if you know what Tracey and I went through together.* I hope the waves of suffering will remind you that you are not alone in your suffering and that somehow, God is with us in it.

By May 8th, Tracey had a high fever, and we returned to the hospital in Memphis. Our fears were confirmed—her appendix was still leaking. Her general surgeon performed a late-night surgery that took seven hours. Eric had been with me through the night, prayed for me at 5am, and had to get back to Oxford. We both cried. The result? A large section of the small bowel was removed, the appendix was "obliterated," and there was now a large vertical incision above the C-section incision. I knew after this we weren't going home any time soon. Before the procedure, the doctor had promised Tracey could go home by Mother's Day. He could not keep that promise anymore. When Tracey figured out that she wouldn't get to go home, I know she just about gave up.

On the Saturday night before Mother's Day, Tracey had a terrible dream that really disturbed her. We watched a beautiful sunrise on Mother's Day and then Tracey went back to sleep. It had to be one of the most disappointing days for Tracey. We thought we could be home celebrating with our church family and Miles in our arms. Instead, we were in the Memphis hospital again, Miles was in Oxford, and there was no end in sight to come home. This surely led Tracey to the brink of despair. In fact, she later described the days as simply "death." I realized how bad it was when her parents brought Miles up to see us. Tracey was unaffected. I remember her mostly sleeping—no smiles, no joy. Miles became my gift of hope and renewal that allowed me to continue to love and give Tracey hope and light, but she seemed beyond hope. When they left, our room became lifeless and quiet again.

A few days later, however, Tracey stopped sleeping so much. She woke up from her long death dream. She actually talked about her experience. It sounded like she had been in a pit of despair, something so profound and deep that words will never fully describe her experience. She talked about how much it meant for me to be with her. Mostly there were joyful tears, and we shared a sacred sorrow …something Satan was very sorry to see, I'm sure.

We briefly returned home, only to face yet another fever. We had to go back…again. We had another tearful moment. I told her how I needed her and didn't want her to give up. We got our things packed and held each other. We joked a lot on the way back. We talked about the hospital like it was a hotel. I was in awe of Tracey's attitude. Things were, in general, better this time around. Tracey walked every day. She was working hard to eat, which is difficult when you're taking so many antibiotics. I told her how proud I was of her. She gave me one of the most beautiful looks of pride and accomplishment. It was sweet and sad. During this hospital stay, my parents brought Miles to Memphis, and it was redemption for Mother's Day. Tracey wanted to hold him and feed him from the beginning.

On the last day of May, an MRI revealed a pocket of liquid in the abdomen, and we feared the worst. Thankfully, on the same day, I remembered the gift basket the church had given us but had left in the car. As we opened the cards, we were inundated with love and prayers. It was so important that God gave us that encouragement when we needed it most. That night I also read Psalm 13 for us, and it became our anthem of lament— How long, O Lord? I was thankful we could grieve the bad news and still go on waiting, hoping, laughing, and eating. But still, that nagging question threatened our joy: how long?

The doctors decided they wanted to avoid surgery, but it came at a high price—four WEEKS of no food by mouth. During this time, Tracey and I walked outside the hospital for the first time, and I pushed her IV pole which she was still bound to with medications. I wish I had a picture of that because it was a beautiful picture of our marriage forged in the fires of all our suffering. Despite it all, we were a team, working together, and suffering together.

After celebrating our 4th anniversary in the hospital, Tracey was stable enough that we felt like we had to get back to Oxford. But she was still not well enough to be at home, so they transferred us to the Oxford Baptist Hospital. At least we were closer to Miles. Speaking of Miles, Tracey's mom, Penny, had dedicated two months almost by herself to caring for Miles but she needed to get back home. It was such a beautiful sacrifice for us, but so hard on her. I had been able to focus on Tracey, sleeping in the same hospital room with her for those two months. After Penny left, I still needed help with Miles. I recall several church families stepping up yet again. The sweet lady who cared for Miles the most was Amy. She loved babies and kids and was always babysitting someone. But she could always take Miles when I needed her. I want to thank everyone here who was the hands of Christ that helped hold and care for Miles when we could not.

Tracey stayed in the Oxford hospital for a month. She was not able to eat for a total of about 30 days. She was getting close to Jesus' territory! By July 19th, Tracey finally left the hospital for good. She still had a small, but persistent wound. (She would have it for another *year* because her body had created a fistula which was basically a new pathway her sick bowel had created that connected to her wound. It was never going to fully heal without surgery.) I had purchased fireworks near July 4th but knew I would save them for whenever she got out. On the night of the 19th, we gathered with some dear students plus Eric and Melanie (elder and wife) to declare Tracey's independence from hospital hell.

I know now that you can appreciate what Tracey and I went through that year—about 3.5 months in two different hospitals and another year after that with an open wound. So much pain and trauma for Tracey; secondary trauma for me. Hundreds of people had prayed and served us; our church family and our elders had supported us through it all. It was only sometime after we were home that Eric said something I don't think I had even considered while Tracey was in the hospital, but now made perfect sense: "She could have died." She was that sick. I thought of these verses from Job 2:4-6: *"'Skin for skin!' Satan replied. 'A man will give all he has for his own life. But now stretch out your hand and strike his flesh and bones, and he will surely curse you to your face.' The Lord said to Satan, 'Very well, then, he is in your hands; but you must spare his life.'"* While it seemed that none of my prayers had been answered the way I wanted, there was one thing God had done—he had spared her life. He did not allow Satan to take my wife from me or Miles' mother from him.[21] I will always be grateful for that; however, there are 42 chapters in Job for a reason. We had just begun to process and lament the injustice of it all—the biggest of which was three and a half months we had missed out on Miles' little life.

Reflect

- *What is your great sadness? If you haven't had a "great" one yet, what is something that has felt far beyond your ability to endure?*

---

[21] I realize that I am speculating here. I don't know for sure that God intervened in any special way, but I am living by faith that he did. I know some of you have lost loved ones and I dare not try and speak to that. I can only speak to how I *think* God was at work in our experience. Paul says something similar in Philippians 2:27.

14

David and Jonathan

Thank you so much for all your help in getting my son moved and settled. He is so happy at the Student Center. I hope you know how much all your work is appreciated. It is too bad every college campus is not able to have one of you for their students!
In Christian love, RFC Mom

Similar to the coffee house, we got the apprentice idea from Tim Stafford and the Memphis ministry. I cannot thank Tim enough for helping me cast vision so early in my ministry. He was training a new generation of campus ministers and that sounded exciting to me. He once said, "Campus ministry is a momentum and inertia kind of thing. If a small leadership group can get started, it will build." I wanted to be part of something that not only helped present-day campus ministry but also the future of campus ministry. This kingdom/mission focus was appealing. Apprentices would work about 25 hours a week while working on a master's degree in ministry. We started by paying $4,000 annually while offering free housing at the Student Center. We would encourage apprentices to raise additional support if they desired. In the fall of 2005, I presented the elders with a proposal for starting an apprentice program to train new campus ministers and they were supportive. This was important to me because my story had not included any practical campus training to go with my great theological training.

Despite the medical craziness of 2006, we still pursued an apprentice to work with us starting in the fall. I probably thought I needed one more than ever to help me bear the burden of family and ministry.[22] We got the word out, especially to the Harding School of Theology (HST) in Memphis. They must have connected us with a student of theirs who was doing youth ministry in Kansas—Lendy Bartlett. He was originally from West Texas. He was a tall guy with that Texas accent who wanted to move closer to Memphis to finish up his degree. He was married to Meagan, and they had a little girl with another one on the way. I cast the vision for Lendy. We wanted to train more campus ministers and would love him to work with us to reach college students at Ole Miss and then someday reach students on another campus. Lendy was more interested in preaching, but it sounded like a great opportunity for him to accomplish his goals. We were ready to get started with someone and took the leap of faith.

He and his family arrived by August, and we began to prepare for the fall. The practical parts of campus ministry were all new to him, but he jumped in with both feet ready to learn and serve. He was the same age as me (28) so we felt more like peers and learned a lot from each other. We quickly became best friends, like David and Jonathan in 1 Samuel 20. We often thanked God for giving us that friendship. Neither of us could have imagined then that we would end up working together in some form or another for eleven years. God really does more than we can ask or imagine. I have always appreciated Lendy's authenticity and vulnerability. He taught a quiet guy like me focused on being a professional minister to still be real and honest about my struggles. The façade of a professional minister can be daunting. It's one of the things I believe Satan tries to use to create a split personality in ministers so that we are one way in public and another way in private. God used Lendy to draw out my weaknesses, my incompetence, in the safety of our friendship so that I could learn to be the same person in public or private.

I included the quote at the beginning because this encouraging mom of an RFC student saw so clearly what I had discovered as well. I couldn't be content that Ole Miss had a good campus ministry. I wanted to help ensure there would be campus ministers at other schools someday because of the training they received with us. It was such a clear indication to me that we were making disciples.

---

[22] We actually had a female apprentice as well and she blessed RFC and especially our women before moving back home after one year. Thank you, Stephanie, for your service to our students.

P.S. **June 2007**: *"Lendy encouraged us to do a fear inventory in his lesson. So, I did one:*

1. *Fear of death—Miles, Tracey, me*
2. *Fear of conflict*
3. *I am afraid of criticism*
4. *I fear the church liking Lendy more*
5. *I fear that I'm not as good a teacher/preacher as I think I am.*
6. *I fear having to leave Oxford"*

Reflect

- *Who was one of the first disciples (interns or apprentices) you trained?*

- *Who has God put in your life so you can safely share your weaknesses?*

- *How different are you in public and private settings?*

- ***Resource:*** *Nate Larkin, Samson and the Pirate Monks*

15

Letter From a Shepherd

"I am glad I can have complete confidence in you." 2 Corinthians 7:16

Kenny Coleman was one of the five original elders who hired me. I got to know all our elders better, including Kenny, when our leadership team traveled for *Elder Link* in 2005. It was great getting to relate to them outside of our more formal leadership meetings. I remember students saying the same thing about me when we went on trips. I will never forget Kenny and Ernie (another elder) laughing uncontrollably as Ernie told "the frozen monkey" story from his days at Oklahoma State. Where was the iPhone when I needed it? Kenny was intimidating at times because we were so different. He was an on-the-go businessman who focused a lot on real estate development in the Oxford area. He seemed to know everybody in town. But after the trauma of 2006, it was special to receive this note from him in June 2007. This is the day he went from being just an elder of my ministry to a shepherd of my heart.

"Dear Casey,

We are so blessed to have you, Tracey, and Miles as a vital part of God's family here in Oxford. It's very clear to me that you have the heart of a servant, and that you are committed to using the gifts God has given you (which are many) in service to Him."

He concluded the letter by talking about hearts and personalities and compared me with his son.

"I learned I can't use the same gauge to determine what is appropriate to say to a tender heart like Glenn's, that may be needed to use on an old crusty heart like mine. We are two distinct personalities. I don't want to change him. God made him the way

he needs to be. His naturally soft, compassionate, tender heart is what makes him so good at dealing with grieving families. Your heart, Casey, is much like that and I want to respect the gifts God has given you and work <u>with</u> you."

I know that was a watershed moment for Kenny and me. I liked that he thought in terms of crusty and soft hearts and was thankful he could see my heart, respect my gifts, and work with me. I know it can be hard and take time but feeling like I was a partner with the elders and not just an employee was a big deal. I think I became like another son to him after that. It made me think of Paul and Timothy's relationship.

I valued Kenny's and Doug Sr.'s thoughts as father and grandfather in the faith so I appreciated these behind-the-scenes insights I recorded soon after that note:

"Three days later, Kenny called to talk more. He said he hoped we'd stay in Oxford until I was grey. And he mentioned how Doug Sr. told him back when they were trying to hire me to do whatever they had to do to get me. Could be a boost to my ego but I'd rather it be an encouragement and a memory I hang on to as I minister here through ups and downs. God, thank you for the sometimes crusty, sometimes soft heart of Kenny and thank you for Doug and his ministry here and support of me."

The business model bleeds into the church often (for better and for worse), but I wonder what would happen if more shepherds saw their young staff ministers first as sons or daughters in the faith and second as employees? I met with Eric most weeks where he worked as a doctor. We would usually have the cafeteria lunch together and talk about ministry and life. It became too numerous to count over the years how many coworkers asked, "Is this your son?" We would always smile and laugh a little. Eric and I did have similar body types and hair lines. I knew I was becoming a son to Eric, but it was nice to feel that bond with other shepherds too like Kenny. It helped me to trust my elders and gave us a chance to have complete confidence in each other.

Reflect

- *What is your relationship with your elders, Board or staff like? Do you feel more like an employee or a son/daughter? What can you do to make the relationship more familial?*

16

Wish You Were Here

I knew other campus ministries were doing this, so early on I caught a vision for taking our students on spring break trips. It seemed like a countercultural alternative for those students who didn't want the traditional college spring break experience. It felt Spirit-led that I reconnected with Jason in West Virginia, and he was happy to host us and give us some evangelistic training on his campus. We saw it as a great benefit to both our ministries for at least three reasons:

1. We stayed in church members' homes which led to strengthening the bonds and memories they had of campus ministry.
2. The West Virginia students were encouraged to see other Christians on a state-school campus who were like-minded, willing to travel, and eager to get on their campus to share faith. We know this helped spur them on.
3. Our students got to experience another campus and practice some things that we could bring back and try on our campus. It was a great evangelistic experiment.

The peak of our travel time was singing "Country Road" with Lendy as we passed into West Virginia. Upon our arrival on campus, we could tell we were no longer in the Bible belt. We went out two-by-two and prayer walked the campus. Part of the time we just walked and prayed quietly. Part of the time, we would try and engage students and see if we could pray for them. Jason had a great project where we set up in one of the "free speech" zones with two tables and long bulletin board pieces of paper. On one we asked, "What do you think about Jesus?" and on the other "What do you think about the church?" There were many great comments. Most were positive about Jesus while many were negative about the church. We had a great discussion later reflecting on people's comments. This was something we took back to Ole Miss and did on campus. One of the comments written by a West Virginia student has stuck with me all these years. She wrote, "Wish you were here." to the question about Jesus. My heart still hurts when I think about this because it's just pure, honest desire. We could, of course, rationally and theologically talk about how Jesus still lives in us or that someday we will see him face-to-face. But I think this moment was more of a lament. We wish Jesus had come during our time on earth. We wish he was here now in a human body dealing with the problems of our world. Sometimes, many times, walking by faith is hard.

We went back to West Virginia the next year. The main thing we did differently was free hugs on campus where we held up signs saying (you guessed it), "FREE HUGS." We offered to hug students and strike up conversations.[23]

I loved that we could engage the campus with:
1. Simple, powerful questions to promote discussion,
2. Gentle prayer requests,
3. Unconditional displays of love in free hugs.

I still think these kinds of things would translate well on most campuses and in most communities, but at least it gave me a different and beautiful alternative to my previous understanding of evangelism. I also like to imagine the conversations that were had the rest of that day or week as students told of their experience: "I saw these people giving out free hugs." "So I got hugged by a stranger today." "This group was asking questions about Jesus and the church." "What do I think about Jesus and the church?" These weren't just one-time events but catalysts for the Spirit to keep working after we were gone.

P.S. **March 2008**: *"Eric restored my integrity while I was gone on spring break trip to West Virginia. Someone thought I was taking naps during work—I took one nap on a vacation day while Miles was in the hospital. I believe this was an issue because I took a nap at the Student Center. Remember what Tracey had already been*

---

[23] Here's the video if you want to check it out:
https://www.youtube.com/watch?v=baMp3KFopoE

through and now we were with Miles in the hospital battling pneumonia at 18 months old. Can't take a nap at the Student Center anymore. So much for grace."

P.P.S **February 2012**: *"I am imagining a time when Miles helped with free hugs. He would hold the sign, hold out his arms, and do what I did. God, help me to see myself as Miles helping his dad. I am but a tiny servant in the kingdom, but that's just the kind of person you want to use."*

Reflect

- *What would you write about Jesus and the church? What might a skeptical friend write? What do you think about doing a similar event on your campus or in your community?*

17

Another Great Sadness

"We are hard pressed on every side but not crushed…" 2 Corinthians 4:8

It was August 2007. Lendy and I had just gotten back from the campus ministry conference at Lipscomb. I got the call from Bob, our preaching minister, on a Friday in my office. Brian Dahl, son of Eric and Melanie, was dead. We were almost the same age. I was in shock and sick to my stomach. I called Tracey. All I could remember was her saying, "No, no, no" in disbelief. Brian had come through so much by beating cancer at a young age. I was there when he rang the bell completing his chemo treatments. He was addicted to cycling and in the best shape of his life. His mental health was better than ever after struggling for years with depression. Brian loved the TV show Monk (Tony Shaloub played an obsessive-compulsive detective), and we watched a few episodes together because Tracey and I loved it too. I can still hear his laugh. Then it hit me…Eric and Melanie. Like Tracey, all I could think was, "No God, no." I remember listening to Eric pray the most gut-wrenching prayer I have ever heard when we went to their house soon after the news. I had the honor to struggle through singing a few songs at the funeral. A painfully beautiful song by Chris Rice simply called "Untitled Hymn" was played over the speakers. Again, the Costons and Dahls were knit together closer than ever by grief.

Somehow by September, we were ready as a ministry to reach the campus. I guess I had to compartmentalize Brian's death just to function. I'm not sure what happened to my weekly meetings with Eric during this time. We at least stayed close through texts and short calls. It was hard carrying around an experience that did not directly impact the students I was working with or trying to reach. With the courage and training we had received in West Virginia, we got on our campus and asked people what they thought about Jesus and the church for several hours. Similar to our time in West Virginia, students' statements about Jesus were shorter and more favorable, while church statements were longer and more critical. Students who sat near us for a long time seemed curious. I wish I had gone over and talked to them. It got easier asking students to share their thoughts the more we did it. We'll come back to that later.

By the next spring, Tracey and I planted a beautiful maple tree in Brian's honor in our yard next to Miles' tree. We placed a simple reflective plaque on stone and laid it in front of the tree. The words on the plaque read:

"In Honor of Our Brother
Brian Dahl
Until We Meet Again at the
Tree of Life"

I still have a picture of Eric, Melanie, and Brian's grandmother, Elza, with the tree. Eric and Melanie began to reenter some semblance of normal life, though they could never go back to normal. Eventually, they made plans to honor Brian's life with an annual bike ride that started in 2011. They connected the event with the Christian Relief Fund (CRF) and raised money to support kids in Haiti and Uganda. The bike ride went on for about seven years. By the end, the event was raising enough money to care for 30 kids annually. It was amazing. It was a tangible way Eric had held God to his promise to work for good in a tragedy.

Reflect

- *What is a tragedy that has affected you indirectly?*

18

Learning to Pray More

"Devote yourselves to prayer, being watchful and thankful." Colossians 4:2

Fall 2005: "Reading 24/7 prayer book. Longing to pray more. Want a prayer room at UCSC."

Ask any follower of Jesus—we all have this nagging feeling that we should be praying more. "Praying more" is tricky for us. We genuinely do want to devote more of our time to prayer but in our fast-paced work culture where busyness is a symbol of our success, we also have this nagging feeling that prayer is not productive work and so not nearly as important as actually doing the work of ministry. I remember one of my ACU professors calling prayer and solitude "wasting time with God" and I was fascinated.[24] It's not natural for our flesh to slow down, be still, and trust that God is mysteriously at work in ways we cannot quantify with our modern metrics.

To help our ministry pray more, part of the new vision I had cast for our Student Center was a prayer room. I had read a great book called *Red Moon Rising* where a movement of 24/7 prayer was occurring in Europe. I was enthralled by the stories told in the book—how young people were committing hours to prayer in a room with their friends. I had never heard of anyone getting this excited to pray. I went about creating a space for prayer. There were four stations so you could spend about 15 minutes at each station and fill an hour of prayer. It made it seem manageable for many of us who

---

[24] Klaus Issler, *Wasting Time with God*, Westmont: IVP, 2001.

had hardly ever prayed for fifteen straight minutes, much less an hour. These were the four stations:

1. Invitation—There were several books on prayer and our devotional life to prompt prayer.

2. Meditation—I had commissioned my uncle to create a large painting of Jesus in the Garden of Gethsemane. I must admit it was intense to see Jesus agonizing in prayer with the soldiers on the way to arrest him, but it was stunning to behold. The city of Jerusalem and the temple were in the background. The point was to learn to tell God what you wanted but to finish with "not my will but yours be done."

3. Confession—There was a cross where you could anonymously nail your confessed sins.

4. Mission—There was a large wall with chalkboard paint so you could write prayer requests for yourself and others. I had heard Randy Harris at the 2006 Gulf Coast Getaway (GCG) say, "What if we prayed for the lost as we prayed for the sick?" It was a wonderful question that built on our deep commitment to pray for the sick but nudged us to consider how we might pray for the lost with the same kind of commitment.

I believe the prayer room was used a lot between 2008-2012. These were the years where we got in a good rhythm inviting students and church members to take an hour so we could fill a full 24 hours with prayer. It was really special to go in the middle of the night and take over for someone who had just been in there. You knew God was the only one who was normally awake at that time, but you were joining him for the sake of the mission to Ole Miss. I marveled at the dedicated disciples who would take a sweet hour for prayer. I don't recall ever struggling to fill up a 24-hour prayer time. It was also special that I had found something that students and church members could participate in together. This would be a common critique of my ministry at times—that church members and students were not together. So, this was a big victory for a season.

The prayer room did lose interest and effectiveness at some point. I know that my family life changed drastically in 2012, which I will talk more about later. I should have delegated more to keep it going. I know most people prayed alone. I should have encouraged more people to pray in small groups so they could share the experience with friends like in the book.

I included this chapter because we desperately need to help our students pray and learn to pray. Plus, there's nothing that binds us together better as the body of Christ than praying for a common purpose. Colossians 4 invites us to be devoted in prayer and devotion is the only thing that can overcome Satan's many distractions. A prayer room may be outdated now, or you don't really have any space for a prayer room, but please, seek out any way you can to help students, and your church pray for the campus they say they want to reach in the name of Jesus. Somehow, God will answer.

Here are some confessions of students written on the prayer room cross.

1. *Father, take away my grief and pain. Why do I allow the sorrow of losing my parents to consume me? You are my parent and I don't want to forget that. So take me in Lord.*

2. *I have let the lust and porn take over again. I have willfully rejected you and mocked the sacrifice you made for me. I have thrown your love back in your face. Jesus forgive me.*

3. *Please forgive me for being afraid about my future. I know you tell me not to be afraid. You will do me no harm. I need to be strong, take heart, and wait for your mighty and amazing work.*

4. *Remember not the sins of my youth and my rebellious ways. I love you, Yahweh.*

Here's a confession of mine from **March 2010:** *"Abba Father, I know that as a leader in a church, I am not leading enough in the area of prayer. Part of me is still not sure my prayers matter. Forgive me. I want to try again to be more faithful in prayer. Satan seems to do his best work in distracting me or making me just tired enough to not pray. I planned to start praying this morning and somehow, I woke up late."*

Reflect

- *What positive and negative experiences have you had with prayer personally or in a group? What do you think is a good idea to get students praying?*

- ***Resource:*** *Pete Greig, Red Moon Rising*

19

Pruning Incompetence

"I am the true vine, and my Father is the gardener. He cuts off every branch in me that bears no fruit, while every branch that does bear fruit, he prunes so that it will be even more fruitful." John 15:1-2

September 2006: *"God, you are the reason for my joy, my peace, my love. You are so beautiful if I would look upon you, if I could catch a glimpse of your glory, then I would know my place, my purpose. I would know better what to say and when to be alone, or when to say 'no' or 'yes.' I could be moved by love, not by frustration or busyness or a selfish will. God, I wish I could be overwhelmed by your light...light so pure, so attractive, and yet it repels because my eyes cannot endure it. The light flows through Christ too and ironically shines the brightest in his wounds...the holes made and left by evil now reveal the light of the gospel. I know this life is at work in me because I hurt and have compassion on the least...the uncool and wimps because that's where I was and still am in many ways. Nobody is labeling me as cool or strong. Maybe I really am one of the foolish things God can use to shame the wise."*

In my early years (I'll guess 2004-2010), I was given a growth review at the end of the year. I believe it was the growth review developed by Dr. Charles Siburt at Abilene Christian University (ACU). I liked Dr. Siburt, though I only had one class with him at ACU. But man, I did not like his growth review. It felt like an annual reminder of my incompetence. I was evaluated by my church elders, fellow ministers, a few interested church members, and maybe even a few students. That's approximately ten voices right there. That also means ten different perspectives on my ministry were combined into my annual review. Ten people with varying degrees of expectations about what I was doing well and what I needed to work on. Ten people with varying degrees of knowledge about my day-to-day work. Ten people. It was an overwhelming and at times traumatizing experience. I don't think I would have survived it or the ministry itself without Eric walking me through it and offering some comfort, support, and nuance.

Let me make two points here. First, hardly anything in life had prepared me for this kind of criticism. My parents were not micromanagers and let me figure a lot of things out on my own. Music and engineering had come relatively easy to me. Even when I was critiqued in grad school by my professors, it was mostly encouraging with just a few things to consider or change. However, these were not highly relational evaluations. And therein lies the tension. My evaluations had switched from *quantitative* to *qualitative*. How do you evaluate someone's teaching when everyone has a different perspective, experience, and standard? Some may want more outward emotion. Some may want three clear points. Some may want a personal story. Some think a personal story makes it too much about me. How do you evaluate someone's effectiveness with students when some will inevitably connect with you more easily than others? How do you take into account my natural strengths, weaknesses, and gifts along with their strengths, weaknesses, and gifts? Second, I can understand why ministers quit after my experience with a growth review. I was disheartened and discouraged and there was no way to have a conversation with the people who made their comments because it was anonymous. Some of that is understandable. I wouldn't want to have a conversation with ten different people. Something is lost in the process, however, when I cannot have a face-to-face conversation about something that impacts how I see myself and my ministry. When some comments stick with you and you have no outlet for nuance or a chance for clarity, there is no growth for the commentators either. I wanted them to understand where I was coming from, see the bigger picture, and at the very least be more patient with me.

At the time it was hard, but I can easily admit now that critical comments made it feel like people didn't understand me or like me or didn't think I was doing a good job. I can admit that I am a people pleaser and tend to be sensitive and take things too personally. I certainly learned that about myself in this process. You could say that I just needed to toughen up and I would mostly agree. But I know that sensitivity is also what makes for a good minister who cares for students. It was like my sensitivity expressed in compassion and pastoral care for students was now being used against me. All of this was hard for me to grapple with as a young minister.

So, in the following comments, I want you to get a feel for what it was like. I will share a few comments in parentheses if I think it is helpful. My reason for sharing all of this is to help you see yourself in my weaknesses, so be honest about your weaknesses and let God prune you as needed for further kingdom growth.

Here's part of my growth review from 2009.

1. *Be careful to value tradition when appropriate.* (I did not consider myself radical in this area, but I did want to take to heart Jesus' words about the danger of tradition in Mark 7.)

2. *Leadership—his delegation skills and empowerment skills could be improved. His ideas fall through due to implementation problems.*

3. *Management—he struggles with ideas that conflict with his own and fails to capitalize on others' strengths and ideas.* (Ouch!)

4. *Make sure and love everyone equally even when you disagree with students' choices and allegiances.* (I certainly prided myself on loving everyone, but in those early years I am sure I struggled with this. It is still easier for young and old professional ministers to gravitate towards like-minded people.)

5. *Give frustration to God not students when they choose something other than campus ministry and discipleship.* (This one was very wise and something I took to heart. I had been guilty of this in my early years and wanted to take it to the Lord in prayer, not take it out on students. A lot of this was an unspoken pressure by others and myself to focus on numbers.)

6. *Try and work as hard on Wednesday lessons as sermons.* (Ouch. Some of this was true. It was easier for me to give more time and energy to a message designed for 250 people versus a message for 50 students. But it was also hard to teach as well on the weeks when I had a sermon to prepare PLUS maintain regular meetings with students. Honestly, something has to give sometimes.)

7. *Be willing to connect with students through deep involvement. Be willing to stay and talk and listen longer. Be interruptible.* (Again, great advice. But after Tracey's health issues, it was a constant struggle to figure out how long to stay and when I needed to get home. I wanted to stay longer most of the time, but balancing family and ministry is a never-ending tension.)

8. *Be careful that willingness to meet is not just a show. Listen and make sure others don't leave more exasperated.* (This one hurt because I didn't feel like I did anything for show. However, I do know it can be hard for me to implement other's ideas. If there is no immediate change, I can understand how it appears to be a show even though it is not. Comments like this were hard to hear because I didn't know the context.)

9. *Communication skills are hurt by passive/non-confrontational personality.* (I was naturally non-confrontational and I'm sure I shied away from conflict at times. I know that I grew in this area over time.)

10. *I think the campus ministry needs more outreach and evangelism. Casey is an extremely gifted minister, though I think his gifts lean more toward running/guiding an established ministry rather than building/rebuilding a small ministry.*

There was more but I'll stop there. There is some truth to almost all of these. I was young and needed to grow. Pruning is a painful, but necessary part of discipleship as John 15 indicates. The thing I struggled with the most was how to implement needed change. One of my favorite images is of the performer on stage who starts spinning plates on a pointy piece of metal. They have to keep coming back to the previous plates as they add more plates. It is amazing how they can keep 5-10 plates going. And of course, at some point, they can no longer keep all the plates spinning and some of them fall and break. I felt like I was working a job where I was being asked to keep ten plates spinning, but I was only good at keeping five going.

Besides Eric's counsel and comfort, our preaching minister, Bob, helped me process the process. One of the best things he suggested was to simplify the growth review. He suggested evaluations every 6 months with two questions:

1. Name one thing you want me to do more because it's helpful.

2. Name one thing you want me to do less because it's not helpful.[25]

Wow. Talk about simplifying the process. This gave me the chance to focus on 1-2 things at a manageable time. Getting a growth review once a year of

---

[25] Whatever timeframe works best for you (quarterly, six months, end of fall and spring semesters, or annually), I would recommend requesting these two questions be used in your review from a small, trusted group of people who know the most about you and the ministry (maybe 3-5 people). If you review others, use the same questions and give them a timeframe.

twenty or more comments with some truth to them was overwhelming and made it really hard to figure out where to start and how to change.

As early as 2006, I was being honest about my incompetence.

September 2006: *"Let go of pride. Let go of forceful ministry—I know I run ahead of God sometimes trying to force my will on students instead of offering God's relentless love."*

November 2007: *"Based on my growth review: I am not perfect. I have weaknesses. I cannot please everybody. I will be misunderstood. I can grow!"*

But the persistent feelings of incompetence lasted about EIGHT years. There was this huge disconnect between what I had been trained to do at ACU versus managing a large complex ministry system. Much of what I did at ACU was learn the Bible well, be formed by it, and be equipped to teach and preach it in small and large group settings. My church appreciated that for the most part but also wanted me to delegate better, work harder (when I felt like I was already giving 110%), and be more patient with students and members who disagreed with my perspective (which I admitted was good counsel and something I tried to work on). I also had to juggle the preferences and personalities of 50-75 students every year, 5-8 church members who were more invested in the ministry, and 10-15 people in leadership counting staff, elders, and student leaders. I just wasn't trained very well to do this.

Soon after a growth review in January 2010, I wrote down this quote from Lipscomb professor John Mark Hicks: "Resentment is like taking poison and expecting the other person to die." Ouch. There was always a temptation to resent the words in those growth reviews, but after a few weeks with family over the Christmas break, God would help me start the new year refreshed and ready to focus on my regular work plus try and implement some new things. The problem was that some of the same problems kept coming up year after year and I'll admit it was hard to figure out HOW to change when you have strengths, weaknesses, ingrained habits, and you have to keep doing your regular work while caring for your family. It reminds me of Paul's words in 2 Corinthians 2:16, *"And who is equal to such a task?"*

Reflect

- *Current Minister: What are some memorable growth reviews you've been given?*

- *Future Minister: How good are you at receiving criticism and why?*

- *Using the shorter evaluation mentioned by Bob in this chapter, ask a trusted friend or mentor to give you some feedback.*

20

A Cord of Three Strands

"A cord of three strands is not quickly broken." Ecclesiastes 4:12

Outside of my training at ACU, I could list several books that have blessed me and helped organize my theology and practice as a follower of Jesus. There were, however, three books in particular that captured my imagination and interest in a way that is hard to quantify. These books were perfect for me and the kind of minister God was training me to be at Ole Miss and beyond. They were the cord of three strands that could not be easily broken.

When you read 1 Corinthians 3, Paul assumed we would build on top of our Jesus foundation. But we need to be careful how we build. These books gave me the materials I needed to build on my foundation. They have only made my faith in Jesus stronger and more focused and have given me a treasure beyond measure that I will explain more at the end of this chapter.

The Reason for God

Obviously, it would take too long to summarize the whole book so I want to give you a taste that might tempt you to go read for yourself. Tim Keller planted a church in Manhattan, New York, in 1989. As you can imagine, he was on the front lines doing Christian mission work in a very skeptical place, but he had tremendous success helping New Yorkers come to faith in Jesus. (Note: Keller didn't start his ministry in New York until he was almost 50 years old. Given that I'm still in my mid-40s, it's mind-blowing to me that his ministry didn't really "take off" until then. God was preparing him behind the scenes in those early years of ministry. So young ministers, please stay humble, be patient, and let God worry about the timing of any success you have in ministry.) It seems to me that if someone is having long-term success helping people outside the Bible belt come to know Jesus, we should take what they are doing seriously. Why? Honestly, because that's where our nation is headed. We have known for years that even young people within churches are leaving their faith for a variety of reasons. It's ok to lament the changes in our society and culture that we perceive are a step away from God or the Christian faith, *but it's not ok to get stuck there*. We have to find a way forward. God is always at work so we must remember that he adapts all the time to ever-changing cultures and systems. He even changed the way he worked between the Hebrew Scriptures and the New Testament.

So, what does Keller address in his book? The first half of the book is given to addressing New Yorkers' response to his question: "What is your biggest problem with Christianity?" You might think that is a strange or even offensive question but if you see yourself as a missionary as Keller does in New York, it is the perfect question. As you might expect, I would argue, that the whole point of the New Testament is for all followers of Jesus to see themselves as missionaries. It is the only way we will reach the world God loves so much. Here are the seven major responses he got from his question, and he devotes a chapter to each:

1. There can't be just one true religion.
2. How could a good God allow suffering?
3. Christianity is a straitjacket.
4. The Church is responsible for so much injustice.
5. How can a loving God send people to hell?
6. Science has disproved Christianity.
7. You can't take the bible literally.[26]

I hope just by looking at that list you are curious and ready to read! You see, most of these are issues that Christians struggle with too, it's just that we have enough faith in Jesus (it only takes a mustard seed!) to give us peace while we search for answers. It's also likely you thought of someone in your circle of influence who you would like to read one of those chapters.

The second half of the book is basically an apologetic defense of Christianity. The thing Keller does so well for a reluctant evangelist like me is

---

[26] Timothy Keller, *The Reason for God*, New York: Riverhead, 2008.

flesh out the Christian apologetic we find in 1 Peter 3:15— "*Always be prepared to give an answer to everyone who asks you to give the reason for the hope that you have. But do this with gentleness and respect….*" He is trying to give people answers, hopeful answers, and he's committed to doing it with gentleness and respect. He's not trying to beat people over the head with a Bible, he's trying to help people understand their background beliefs and how those contribute to where they are in their spiritual journey. This is the heart of a missionary— meeting people where they are. If every Christian did that, we would change the world. Too often, we don't want to give people hope, we just want to hold up a sign telling people what we think--with no gentleness and respect. Others of us are very gentle and respectful but still too afraid to give any answers that might help people find Jesus. We've got to hold together this tension of a hopeful truth spoken in love.[27]

Keller gave me a way forward in my desire to reach seeker students at Ole Miss—giving hope, not hate, with gentleness and respect. It really is the best way to help someone find Jesus.

Mere Discipleship

"At the heart of baptism lies an astonishing claim, an astonishing reality: all the division, all the social groupings, all the forms of identity that serve to categorize, divide, estrange and alienate one from the other—these are broken down."[28]

Lee Camp had spoken at a campus retreat back in my college days since he and my campus minister, Scott, knew each other. He had captured my imagination at the 2007 conference at Lipscomb University in Nashville, talking about the beautiful challenge of following Jesus. I must have picked up his book *Mere Discipleship* soon after the conference. In the fall of 2008, we had Lee do a retreat for us at Ole Miss. It was an election year so the fall was the perfect time to teach it although I knew it would stretch and challenge our students like it did me. You might wonder what an election year had to do with *Mere Discipleship*. You will soon see.

Lee told some painful stories that most of us should have heard. There was the genocide in Rwanda in 1994. Touted as the most Christian nation,

[27] And in the true spirit of a missionary who is always adapting, Keller wrote a new book entitled *Making Sense of God* that compliments *The Reason for God* as an emotional apologetic. I actually have not read this book but have listened to the podcast that is based on the book—**Questioning Christianity**—which I highly recommend for yourself and seekers.

[28] Lee C. Camp, *Mere Discipleship (Second Edition)*, Grand Rapids: Brazos Press, 2008, 152.

the two dominant tribes, the Tutsis and the Hutus, ended up killing each other with total deaths of around 800,000 within a one-hundred-day period. How could such a thing happen where as much as 90 percent of the population claimed some kind of Christian affiliation? *Because tribe was more important than Jesus.* That couldn't happen here, right? We know very well it did in the 1860s when North and South killed each other and 600,000 died. David Lipscomb, a leading Christian preacher in the Nashville area, wanted to know how Southern Christians could kill their Northern Christian brothers. How could Northern Christians make widows out of their Southern sisters in Christ?[29] *Because tribe was more important than Jesus.*

Camp tells a story about Lipscomb that is one of my favorites for imitation: *"During the war, the famed Confederate commander Nathan Bedford Forest sent a soldier to hear Lipscomb preach so that he might judge whether Lipscomb was advocating treason. After the sermon, the soldier remarked, 'I have not reached a conclusion as to whether or not the doctrine of the sermon is loyal to the Southern Confederacy, but I am profoundly convinced that he is loyal to the Christian religion.'"[30]*

This was one of the clearest examples of what I wanted to be as a follower of Jesus. I didn't want to get labeled either left or right. Or if I did get labeled, I wanted it to be coming from both sides. I wanted to keep people guessing about where I stood on their pet issues. Jesus often found a third way of viewing life to get out of the traps laid for him. Jesus had done this on the issues of his day like whether to pay the tax to Caesar or not. I wanted people to know that I was loyal to Jesus. He was Lord of my life and that affected every corner of my heart, every motive, every action.

And so, Camp unpacked Scripture with a bent towards his emphasis on ethics. If Jesus really is Lord, then what does that mean for our lives? Nothing is off limits; nothing can be compartmentalized. Of course, this can be scary practically as we learn to let go of our idols and realize our blind spots, but it makes our witness as followers of Jesus much clearer and more compelling.

Here are a few chapter titles that I hope will pique your interest.

1. Pledging Allegiance to the Kingdom of God
2. Worship: Why Disciples Love Their Enemies
3. Baptism: Why Disciples Don't Make Good Americans
4. Prayer: Why Disciples Trust God rather than Their Calculations

---

[29] Lee C. Camp, *Mere Discipleship (Second Edition)*, Grand Rapids: Brazos Press, 22.
[30] Ibid, 23.

Now you can see the challenge of sharing this in an election year. As followers of Jesus, we owe it to our resurrected Lord to make sure that he has our hearts and that all our other loves in this world are a distant second to him. Otherwise, we are at risk of idolatry and hurting our witness in Jesus' name.

Paul has a great line in 2 Corinthians 10:3-5 that goes well with *Mere Discipleship*: *"For though we live in the world, we do not wage war as the world does. The weapons we fight with are not the weapons of the world. On the contrary, they have divine power to demolish strongholds. We demolish arguments and every pretension that sets itself up against the knowledge of God and we take captive every thought to make it obedient to Christ."* Lee does a great job of critiquing and sometimes demolishing those arguments that should not compete with the gospel.

I want to end this section with the quote below. It doesn't come from Camp's book, but it summarizes much of his book. It captures the heart of why Christianity is stunningly beautiful to those who have ears to hear and terribly threatening to those who don't. *"The paradox of the church was that it was a religious revolutionary movement, yet without a conscious political ideology; it aimed at the capture of society throughout all its strata but was at the same time characteristic for its indifference to the possession of power in this world. Celsus (an early church critic) was the first known person to realize that this non-political, quietist, and pacifist community had it in its power to transform the social and political order of the empire."*[31]

Surprised By Hope

N.T. Wright is a world-renowned New Testament scholar. He has been a great gift to the universal church. I read some of his scholarly work in grad school but it took *Surprised By Hope* for me to really appreciate his insights. Again, I can't really do justice to Wright's book, but I will attempt to tempt you again with some critical points of interest.

1. There is life after death and life *after* life after death.[32] Wright talks about how contemporary Christians have become too focused on life after death—meaning, going to heaven when we die. This is biblical as Paul mentions in Philippians that it would be better for him to depart and be with the Lord.[33] But this view pales in comparison to the major concern of the New Testament, which is

---

[31] Henry Chadwick, *The Early Church (Revised Edition)*, London, Penguin Books, 1993, 69.

[32] N.T. Wright, *Surprised by Hope*, New York: HarperOne, 2008, 36.

[33] Philippians 1:23

life *after* life after death, or the return of Jesus. Paul gives us a great example in Titus 2:13: *"…while we wait for the blessed hope—the appearing of the glory of our great God and Savior, Jesus Christ…."* A narrow focus on us going to heaven when we die takes the emphasis off of Jesus.

2. The resurrection makes the most historical sense for what happened after Jesus' death.[34] Wright goes briefly through many of the counter arguments proposed by opponents and skeptics who rightly struggle to accept the resurrection. I say "rightly" because let's be honest—it should sound crazy that we believe in a God who raises the dead. We have never seen such a thing, but we trust that it's true because we believe that God is speaking through the Bible and believe that it makes the most sense as to what actually happened. Still, it is a mind-blowing revelation that is hard for common sense, scientific people to accept.

3. Jesus had a material body after his resurrection.[35] Jesus tells us in Luke 24:39, *"Look at my hands and my feet. It is I myself! Touch me and see; a ghost does not have flesh and bones, as you see I have."* It seems strange that John is telling us about Jesus eating a piece of fish unless we understand that John is recording for us what the resurrected body of Jesus can do (John 21:10). Ghosts wouldn't eat. Likewise, there is a very strange verse where Jesus comes and stands among the disciples even though the doors are locked (John 20:19). This means Jesus could somehow pass through doors and walls even though he was not a ghost. We have to admit that's kind of freaky and beyond our natural world.

4. We will have a material body like Jesus after our resurrection. There is nothing clearer than Philippians 3:20-21: *"But our citizenship is in heaven. And we eagerly await a Savior from there, the Lord Jesus Christ, who, by the power that enables him to bring everything under his control, will transform our lowly bodies so that they will be like his glorious body."*

5. Whatever it means exactly, there will be a new creation expressed as a new heaven and a new earth. From Isaiah 66 to Romans 8 to 2 Peter 3 to Revelation 21, there are glimpses of the new creation that God intends for all of creation when Jesus returns.

---

[34] Ibid, 53-76.
[35] Ibid.

Even though I had read these passages before, it took Wright drawing my attention to them for the Spirit to give me a second touch like Jesus had done for the blind man in Mark 8. The resurrection had practically made my life more hopeful, which is what God intended for it to do. That's what I wanted to give students and the church as well.

What did these three books have in common? They had all given me HOPE and you can never have too much hope in this dark world. Keller equipped me with a *hopeful apologetic*. He gave thoughtful, respectful answers that helped people get closer to Jesus. Camp gave me a *hopeful discipleship* that wasn't going to get bogged down in the standard culture and political wars. I wasn't going to let anyone pin me down on the left or the right because the only thing that really mattered was a life based on "Jesus is Lord." It is so important to give people this alternative when we think about how much time and money Americans give to an elephant or a donkey when Christians worship a lamb. Finally, Wright gave me a *hopeful theology* that was desperately needed to combat the suffering Tracey and I had experienced and the challenges of learning how to be a campus minister who didn't come to the job as competent as I would have liked. These were the three strands that strengthened my faith in Jesus and would not be easily broken.

Reflect

- *What is a book that has most impacted your spiritual journey? Which one of these would you be interested in reading now?*

21

Attraction Vs. Discipleship

"Since, then, we know what it is to fear the Lord, we try to persuade others."
2 Corinthians 5:11

Milton Jones is a hero in our campus ministry network. He had been a campus minister at Texas Tech before planting a new ministry in Seattle to reach students. I still remember the impact Milton's lesson had on me after the 2005 conference: *"Milton challenged me to change—to stand at the door. I cannot maintain a campus ministry. I must reach out and be sent to campus. We will not minister where we have not prayed. Agonize not organize."* He was so focused on discipleship, and he had the stories to go with it of how lives were changed over the years as disciples of Jesus took his teaching seriously. Milton was, and is, a great storyteller. I remember going up to my campus minister, Scott, after his message feeling burdened for the lost and saying, "We have to do better."

Turning to the 2009 conference, Milton preached on the final day. He had two phrases that I wrote down from his message:

1. "Give yourself to a few people for an extended period of time."
2. "Invest in people and take them as far as you can go."

Then he gave this big illustration composed of 7 concentric circles. He first talked about it biblically. Jesus was in the center. John was the beloved disciple in the next circle. After that was Peter, James, and John. Then it was

The Twelve disciples, the Seventy (sent out in Luke), the 500 who were witnesses to Jesus' resurrection and finally the multitudes. See illustration. [36]

Then there was a modern-day comparison for each one.

1. John => Prayer partner
2. Peter, James, and John => Discipleship group
3. The Twelve => Small group
4. The Seventy => Campus ministry large group
5. The 500 => The local church
6. The multitudes => The University

---

[36] Used by permission from Milton Jones' presentation at the 2009 conference.

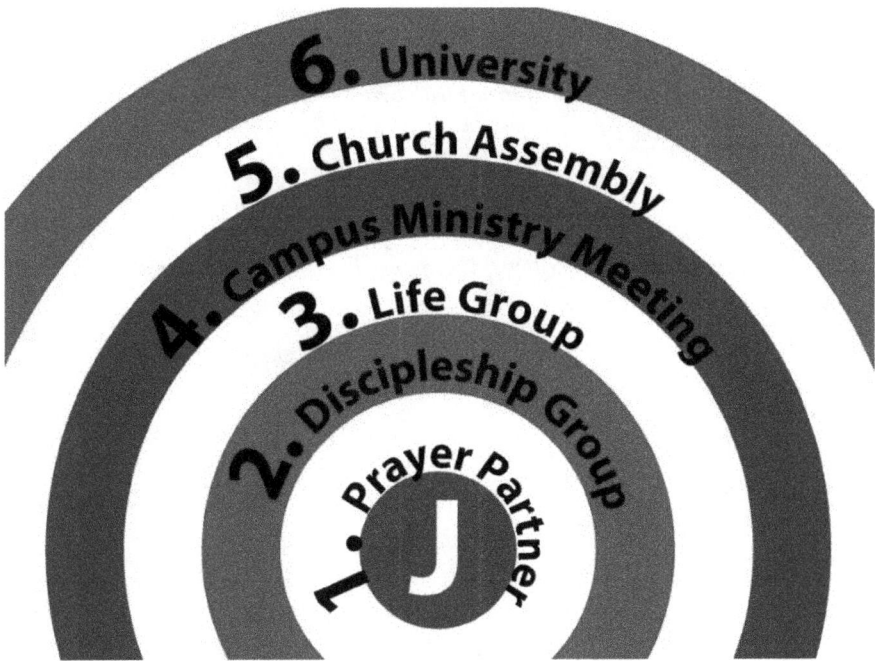

It was a compelling example, even if our numbers were a little different. It wasn't meant to be an exact science, but it did ring true. Then Milton said something that hit deep in my soul: *"Discipleship occurs on 1, 2, and 3. But we devote lots of time to 4, 5, and 6."* This still hits me hard for reasons that will become clearer later. I wish I could say I went home and implemented this immediately, but I did not. Once again, I experienced how hard it is to make personal and systemic changes—especially when so few of my student leaders and elders experienced the same message I had heard. But I did begin to use it. Lendy and Eric were in circle 1. Apprentices were in circle 2. Interns and other student leaders were in circle 3. Still, I spent a vast amount of time focused on attraction ministry—preparing Bible class lessons for Sunday morning and Wednesday night (level 4). I was preaching once a month and helping with worship leading with our church family (level 5). Our outreach events focused on level 6. It was hard to figure out how to cut something from 4, 5, and 6 so I could devote more time to 1, 2, and 3. God did plant a seed, and it did begin to grow, which is the important part, but it would take *ten more years* for me to realize the full implications of Milton's lesson.

Reflect

- *Journal about your experience with circles 1, 2, and 3 versus 4, 5, and 6. What is the tension you feel between attraction ministry and discipleship in your life? Fill out circles 1-6 with the people and groups that would best fit in each circle.*

- ***Resource***: *Milton Jones, Discipling: The Multiplying Ministry (kindle edition)*

22

An Unexpected Complication

"In all our troubles my joy knows no bounds." 2 Corinthians 7:4

In November 2008, Tracey was struggling with not being pregnant again yet. She was feeling alone each month in her sadness, and I wasn't able to connect with her sadness on the same level. I was asking God to grant me a stronger connection to my wife—to let her feed off my joy and contentment and let me lean into her lament.

By April 2009, Trace was feeling pregnant and getting our hopes up. We were starting to imagine her being pregnant near Easter and having a baby near Christmas. She was not pregnant. We had been trying for over a year to get pregnant again with no success. We were beginning to wonder if something was wrong. After all that had happened to Tracey in 2006, NO ONE had told us there could be fertility issues. In **July 2009**, I wrote this: *"Yesterday, we got the bad news we had feared. Trace had a test done and found that both of her fallopian tubes were blocked. I had fasted the day before, we prayed that night, and our elders had been praying for weeks. God did not answer our prayers the way we wanted…again. So now it is impossible to get pregnant. We must now research in vitro fertilization (IVF) to see if we can have kids unless God wants to work a miracle. Trace and I broke down crying when we left the testing site. Lendy sent a text saying he had $3,000 that was ours if needed. We really broke down reading that. How long will you let her suffer, O Lord? Do not let her suffer without hope."*

I should say that the topic of adoption came up a few times, but because Tracey's first pregnancy had ended so abnormally, she really wanted to try and have a normal pregnancy and birthing experience the next time around.

In September 2009, we started our first IVF attempt which ended unsuccessfully. It was a hard process for Tracey with lots of needles and added hormones, but we were just beginning and felt sure it would work eventually.

Reflect

- *What struggles have you and your spouse had getting pregnant or other struggles?*

- *If single, do you want a family? If so, how flexible are you about your plans?*

23

Why Not Preaching?

"We implore you on Christ's behalf: Be reconciled to God." 2 Corinthians 5:20

U nlike youth ministry, it was a lot harder to decide whether or not to consider preaching. For youth ministry, I honestly don't think it was the age group that was the main problem. It was what I perceived, right or wrong, to be the culture of youth ministry. It felt like everything had to be attraction-based, cool, and fun plus there was the variable of working with parents that added to my unease. I knew that wasn't a good fit for me. But I did enjoy studying for a sermon, carefully crafting a lesson, proclaiming it to the church, and getting feedback like this from church members that it was helpful:

"You stepped on my toes and lifted me up at the same time."

"Please pass on to Casey that his lesson yesterday ranks in the top 10 of all lessons that I have ever heard from the pulpit. That may not say much for me, but it was a great lesson on baptism."

Ironically, it feels weird to be good at something you don't feel called to do. I felt gifted at music and had lots of success in music but didn't feel called to pursue a life of music. Similar with engineering. Preaching has been a lot like that for me. I think maybe it's all the other stuff that comes with being a preaching minister that made it less appealing.

Here are three journal entries within a short period where I wrestled with where I could best be used in the kingdom.

September 2007: *"For me, where am I most effective right now? Can God use me more on campus or in the church? He could keep me in campus ministry for a long* *time or equip me for transferring my training to the church. Where do the elders see me in relation to Bob? I've heard several comments about my preaching that confirm some kind of gift there. Am I content preaching once a month? Yes—most of the time. I selfishly think about the money increase…not a good reason. I feel like my time is still in campus ministry for the short term (5+ years). Who knows? What is my purpose, Lord? Where would you have me serve? May Scripture, quiet time, and community provide the answers at just the right time."*

October 2007: *"Why do I preach?*
1. *Like Jeremiah, the word burns in my heart until I speak it.*
2. *Preaching counters the schemes of Satan.*
3. *I believe that with my training, the Spirit, my gifts, and my personality and experience, I offer a unique presentation of the Word.*
4. *I feel affirmed when people say, "I'd never thought about it that way before."*

November 2007: *"I still struggle with my long-term plans…am I meant to be a pulpit preacher sooner, later, never? Am I in the right vocation? I certainly enjoy the campus work."*

A year later, our church came to a critical moment where Bob would slowly begin to transition to retirement, but apparently, I had gotten some clarity and my mind was made up.

October 2008: *"Bob has requested, and the elders have agreed, to design an arrangement that would allow him to gradually transition into retirement. In order to make this transition possible, we will need some help. To gradually relieve Bob of his workload during this transitional period, we want to create a new position on our ministry staff that we are planning to call the associate minister. We have discussed this role with our veteran campus minister, Casey Coston, but Casey has firmly replied that his heart is in Campus Ministry."*[37]

I appreciated the elders consulting with me and have to chuckle a little that at four years I was already a "veteran campus minister." I certainly didn't feel competent enough for that title. Lendy was the one who ended up taking the associate minister role. That felt like a better fit to me. I had seen his passion for preaching and whatever my passion was, it didn't match his.

About seven years went by before I was "tempted" twice in the same year.

---

[37] Words by Doug Shields Jr. included in the Oxford Church of Christ bulletin.

February 2014: *"Got an application from the Meadowbrook Church of Christ in Jackson thanks to a recommendation. Honored but still feel called here. You know I love serving you here and want to make deeper inroads at Ole Miss and beyond through campus planting."*

November 2014: *"It was humbling and encouraging to be considered. It seems like the last time I got the offer to consider Meadowbrook, I was having some challenges in my ministry. Like God or Satan was giving me a way out. Isn't it weird that it's hard to know which? God, I know you are good and all your intentions towards me are good."*

That was two preaching opportunities within about nine months. As you can see, I was trying to make sense of it all. Was God trying to tell me something? Was Satan trying to lure me away? That may sound silly but I'm sure it resonates with any ministers reading this. Sometimes we go through seasons of struggle or ineffectiveness that cause us to wonder whether we are called to endure or if God is giving us a way out. Perhaps either option is ok under the right circumstances. It really takes prayer, wisdom, and discernment with trusted mentors to know what God might be up to. I chose to stay and endure. I remember a few of my peers leaving campus ministry from time to time. I lamented them leaving because it felt like there were so few of us already. Maybe I wanted to stay in part because we were so few.

In March 2019, Meadowbrook had another opening. After looking at the job description, I told Eric this: "It feels like a little too much for me. I think with Tracey and the kids, senior preaching minister is more something I might could do in my 50's. I just feel like fighting for the campus with a small band of disciples rings true to me." I had made my choice and it seemed to get easier the longer I was a campus minister.

Reflect

- *What struggles have you had trying to discern which type of ministry is best for you?*

24

Invitation or Coercion?

Campus ministry, like all ministry, contains a lot of inviting. Normally, you are trying to invite students to one of three groups:

1. Large group: Sunday morning worship, midweek gatherings, etc.
2. Small group: Normally 3-12 students for fun or spiritual purpose (i.e. intramurals, Bible study)
3. One-on-one: Coffee or lunch for getting to know a student better through storytelling and more personalized conversation about questions the student has.

In my early days of inviting, I could only email or call students. Can you imagine calling students today?! Then it grew to texting and social media. I tried to discern what I was inviting students to base on how I met them, who else they knew, and what I knew of their faith.

Students responded in one of four ways and it is interesting how these responses line up pretty well with the parable of the soils in Mark 4:

1. Yes: just set the time and place (good soil)
2. No: It was hard to get a direct "no" from a student because I think they felt guilty (because they knew God, or their parents would want them to accept) so I had to learn to make sure it was ok to say "no." I often failed at this in the first few years. (seed on the path)
3. Maybe: This answer was given almost as often as a "yes." Students are busy with many good and not-so-good opportunities, and it is hard for them to prioritize spiritual things while juggling academic and social interests. (seed among the thorns)

4. Ghosting: Students don't reply at all. Half the time it seemed to be because my text or email got lost in all the other ones. Half the time it was likely intentional because they didn't want to deal with me. We've all done this. (seed on the path)

There is an art to inviting and it takes prayer and practice to get a good feel for how the discernment process works. As you can imagine, over the weeks, months, and years, you get a lot of rejection, intentionally or not. There is the temptation to discouragement, cynicism, and resentment because it can feel like no one is interested in spiritual things. This is surely a scheme of Satan. Below is a song I wrote called "You're Invited" based on Matthew 22:1-14 that speaks to the heart of all invitation and it works well with college students who we must constantly invite and never give up on. It is a minister's joyful responsibility to ring out the invitation because most of the time, at some point, perhaps when you least expect it, they will say "yes"! I confess the alternative, coercion, is tempting because it might temporarily bring us the results we want, but history has shown us groups that have done this with devastating effects to God's kingdom. In the end, it is fake fruit produced by our efforts, not the Holy Spirit. Lord, help us to invite!

<u>Verse 1</u>
You're invited to the table.
You're invited to the feast.
You're invited to the banquet.
Come and sit at Jesus' side!

(Chorus)
Kingdoms will rise and kingdoms will fall
But this kingdom will always be forever
Kingdoms will pass but this kingdom will last
Jesus' death made it always and forever
Empty tomb made it always and forever

<u>Verse 2</u>
You're invited. Don't be busy.
You're invited. No more "no's."
You're invited. Business can wait.
King and Son offer you a plate!

(Chorus)

<u>Verse 3</u>
Share the invite with your friends.
Share the invite with your foes.
God has told us bring good and bad—
Let them be filled, no longer sad.

(Chorus)

Reflect

- *What memories do you have about inviting someone to be part of spiritual things?*

- *What has been the most common excuse? When have you been tempted to use coercion?*

25

Learning to Like Jesus and the Church

"We put no stumbling block in anyone's path so that our ministry will not be discredited." 2 Corinthians 6:3

I do not consider event planning to be a strong suit of mine. I helped organize our welcome week events every fall with the help of apprentices and interns plus we planned the "Feast of a 1000 Chickens"[38] where the church brought a lot of chicken, and we invited college students to join us on a Sunday night. I mostly delegated that to Deborah, our Student Center Manager, while I focused on inviting as many students as I could. But I really wanted to host the four-day 2010 Connect Conference (Now called Campus for Christ). It had been a dream of mine to host because it had blessed me every year and I wanted to be able to do that for others. Plus, I wanted to honor Doug Shields Sr. and celebrate 50 years of campus ministry at Ole Miss—a remarkable kingdom feat! I had been working with my elders to get their blessing to host. I remember they had some reservations given the contextual differences between a local ministry and a national conference (i.e. worship style, role of women, etc.). Thankfully having the conference on campus took away most of those concerns. Plus, the conference board was always gracious about accommodating the local church on Sunday morning where the final gathering occurred. It was also going to be hard to pull off

---

[38] Thanks to Luke Duncan an RFC alum for coining the phrase.

with all the little details that go into an event like this, but I had an ace up my sleeve. I knew that if Kathy Gates was able to help, we could do it. Kathy had been on my search committee and had always been a great encourager and supporter. She was also our RSO (Registered Student Organization) Advisor because she worked on campus. To give you a clue as to her competency, she was part of the team that had helped Ole Miss host the first presidential debate on campus in 2008 between Barack Obama and John McCain, so I knew she could handle our conference. As soon as I asked her, she was all in! Melanie (Eric's wife) was a big help in mobilizing our church family and overseeing a late-night fellowship time at the Student Center, which included hearing about the adventures of great campus ministers and storytellers like Milton Jones and Scott Lambert. Plus, Lendy dressed up like Elvis and sang for us! So even though I wasn't competent to host, I surrounded myself with people who were.

Our main speaker for the conference was Dan Kimball. He had written a very thought-provoking book called *They Like Jesus, but Not the Church*. Dan's material was so foundational to working with college students—evaluating our hearts, motives, and fears. He focused on how the church often undermines or discredits the mission of Jesus. It reminded me of what we had learned on those spring break trips asking students about Jesus and the church. I still remember a great example he gave. Logically, it made sense that the longer we are Christians, the more non-Christian friends we would have. Over time, you became more like Jesus and thus, you would take on his mission to reach the lost. But practically, it was just the opposite. The longer we were Christian, the less non-Christian friends we tended to have.[39] Unwittingly, we began to live in a Christian bubble that kept us from engaging our seeker and skeptic friends. We just hung out with our brothers and sisters in Christ and didn't concern ourselves much with "the one" in Luke 15. That's the "members only" thinking I talked about earlier with our building. He did share some practical advice like:

- Ask lots of questions
- Listen to the concerns of the lost
- Meet them where they are geographically and spiritually

I hope these sound like basic missionary practices, but sadly we often need reminding. He also shared that young adults are to be respected and

---

[39] Dan Kimball, *They Like Jesus but Not the Church*, Grand Rapids: Zondervan, 2007, 43.

given a voice in the church and that mission should be the driving force of the church. I was honored to be acknowledged on stage along with my wonderful team on Saturday night. I actually received a standing ovation from our little band of disciples totaling only 125 people from around the country. The only reason I share that is to tell you that this was one of my purpose moments when every fiber of my being was saying, "This is what I'm supposed to be doing." God was making me competent.

I was able to teach a class on my passion, the resurrection, Sunday morning. Check out Appendix A for the main points. Tracey produced yet another wonderful digital photo album of the event with the Casting Crowns song "Until the Whole World Hears." She ended it beautifully with a picture of a window in the room where Dan spoke. He had challenged us to put the name or names of people we wanted to see come to Jesus on a sticky note and then we went and stuck it on that window. There were about 100 sticky notes on the window representing those people we longed to see give their lives to Jesus. When we all saw that final image on the screen, we knew that our mission was to go back to our campuses and share Jesus until the whole world hears.[40]

The conference was a turning point in my ministry for sure. I was starting to feel like God was making me competent. It seemed fitting that just a couple of weeks after the conference, on August 15th, I was encouraged by these words I had journaled: *"Doug Sr. said tonight that I am likely the longest serving campus minister at Ole Miss. 50 years of campus ministry at Ole Miss and the longest period anyone has served is six years—hard to believe. Sad because a ministry needs roots and stability. Happy for me to know that I have stayed and endured for a few years now. And maybe bring Doug some joy in knowing that God is still using his vision for campus ministry. Help me, Lord. Can't do this without you."*

Reflect

- *How does Kimball's book title resonate with your experience? Have a conversation with 2-3 seekers and skeptics about their perception of Jesus and the church.*

---

[40] Check out the 2010 conference video here:
https://www.youtube.com/watch?v=MdQcQiVy0YY

26

Whiplash

"Perplexed, but not in despair..." 2 Corinthians 4:8

Given all that Tracey had been through, I felt she had a legitimate claim to disability benefits. We wrestled with the decision to proceed and rightly so, but reluctantly decided to go through the process and let God decide. On Miles' 2010 birthday, we had our court hearing for Tracey's disability claim. We thought it was a little strange and perhaps providential that it happened on his birthday. Four years had passed since all the pain began and our lives changed forever. The joy of Miles' birth had always been mixed with the sorrow of Tracey's health struggles. Our hope was that we would experience a little bit of mercy and justice after all Tracey had been through. We'd had so many medical bills to pay. This would certainly help us take care of some of our financial struggles.

A month later we got the news that we were awarded disability benefits. We were in joyful shock. We took Eric and Melanie, Lendy and Meagan out to eat to celebrate. They had known the most and suffered with us the most those four years. It was so sweet to share the abundance with them.

About the same time, Tracey had started her second IVF attempt. She did her test in Birmingham, driving a total of 6 hours to take a 5-minute test. She received the call as she arrived back at home—she was pregnant! What wonderful and scary news! I knew I would feel better after future tests. I wrote this prayer in my journal: *"Great God, we praise you for working powerfully in Tracey's body—we know you oversaw this process to make sure we might experience redemption! Thank you for being so good to us. This is all so overwhelming. We love you and want to declare your praise."*

You know those moments you've watched on TV or in a movie when people look happy but the ominous music alerts you that something bad is about to happen? We were too happy to hear the music. A week later a second test told us it was a chemical pregnancy which basically meant the first was a false positive. We were devastated by the emotional whiplash. How cruel to think Tracey was pregnant and then to not be. How long, O Lord? But I was encouraged to see Tracey growing in her faith. We were praying almost every night, and she had a soft heart toward God. It wasn't long before we were trying again. Thanks to the disability funds, it was just a matter of recovering emotionally and getting ready to try again. I was anxious about trying again close to the fall semester, but Tracey had been so supportive of my work hosting the conference that it felt like one of those things I just needed to get over and trust God to work it all out.

By mid-September, we had confirmed another failed IVF attempt and more waiting for God to redeem us from the pit. Now we were emotionally spent, and I still had to face the fall semester with students. It was hard to make sense of why it seemed to us like God had blessed us with this money so we could go through IVF, but we had no children to show for it. It reminded me of that time in Arkansas when I received all those scholarships and I thought that was a sign to stay in engineering. I was wrong about that, so what was God up to? It was a dangerous time spiritually and our marriage was fragile. Thankfully, we had invited Milton Jones to join us that fall, and it was just the boost I needed. But I was beginning to worry that nothing short of more children was going to satisfy Tracey.

Reflect

- *Do you know anyone who has been on disability? What was your perception of them?*

27

Ripple Effects

"Our hope is that, as your faith continues to grow, our sphere of activity among you will greatly expand." 2 Corinthians 10:15

Having Milton in Oxford for the summer conference made it easy to invite him back in October to have a special night for Rebels for Christ (RFC). I had no idea how special it would be and the ripple effects that would flow out of us hosting the conference. I knew Milton was the godfather of campus ministry to many of us in our tribe. I learned it was due in large part to him having planted a ministry in Seattle and had helped many people discover Jesus during that time—like a West Coast Tim Keller. Previously, I had heard him speak at the conference, been convicted by his lessons, and admired him from afar. Now I had a real relationship with him and got to talk with him about life and ministry. The myth had become a real man. On the night Milton spoke, we encouraged everyone to be ready to donate a few dollars so that we could begin sponsoring a child with the Christian Relief Fund (CRF) which was their primary ministry. It took $35/month to care for one child. Providentially, Milton had been to Haiti at the beginning of 2010 because of a terrible earthquake. He told us children and families had been bused north to Cap Haitien away from the destruction around the capital city of Port au Prince. He also talked about the need for clean water because of the cholera epidemic which was a consequence of the earthquake.

By the end of the night, we had raised over $1,200 so we could sponsor three children, two of which were in Haiti. Two of our student leaders picked the children and I remember how excited they were to show me who they had picked. We also started making plans that night for a mission trip the next summer to Haiti—the poorest country in the Western hemisphere. We wanted to see the work there and bring them some clean water if we could by raising $3,000 for two filtration systems. It was an amazing night. It made me realize that being part of the kingdom and connecting with God's work around the world was passion-producing and door-opening! After finals in December, the Haiti team stayed in town for five days to work jobs that our church family would donate for. We raised $2,000 in five days—amazing! And it all started by hosting the conference. God was blessing us and giving us a core group of students who were getting a global kingdom vision for how he was at work and wanted us to participate.

Reflect

- *What has been a special event that was a catalyst for your ministry?*

- **Resource:** *Consider inviting Milton/CRF to come speak at your ministry or ask them to help you get a mission trip planned. (https://crf.com/go)*

- **Respond:** *Visit crf.com and sponsor a child, individually or as a group!*

28

Marriage on the Rocks

"If we are comforted, it is for your comfort, which produces in you patient endurance of the same sufferings we suffer." 2 Corinthians 1:6

In mid-March 2011, Tracey had her 4th IVF cycle pregnancy test. It was not good news…again. A quick google search shows that there is no conclusive evidence that the strain of IVF impacts the divorce rate. But there is an indication that divorce rates do go up IF fertility treatments do not produce a child. I remember vividly our feelings but not many other details on the day we found out about our failed fourth attempt. In my heart, I was done, but I didn't know how to tell Tracey that. I wanted this for her really bad which is why I was willing to go through it four times. I wanted more kids too but not as much as her. I could clearly see that. When Tracey started immediately talking about trying again, I knew we were in trouble. I wanted her to grieve without trying to talk about the future, but the present grief was too much to bear. We had a brief, heated argument. I don't recall us talking much that weekend. Tracey had barricaded herself in our bedroom. I remember thinking this could really lead to divorce. We were in a very scary, dark place. From the beginning, when we had considered getting married in a hospital, our marriage had been anything but normal. We tried to balance our belief that all marriages usually have some tough times with the fact that our marriage felt freakish. We were going on year five of tough times with no end in sight.

God used Miles to help us start talking again after the weekend. He had gone to our bedroom door and knocked. Tracey let him in and he said,

"Mama, why won't you let me in with your sadness." The door of her heart had been opened by a four-year-old. We also reached out to Eric and Melanie to come over and help us. Spring break was near, and we decided to go visit my parents and get away from all the IVF sadness. My parents took good care of us. Still, on the drive back to Oxford, grief and fear crept back into our hearts. We were scared to talk about anything important. Tracey was too emotional, and I was too rational. We couldn't figure out how to work together. We were stuck. A few weeks later we had to register Miles for kindergarten which was very hard on Tracey—contemplating an empty, quiet house.

Thankfully, we started counseling. John Kennedy was our counselor. Our church elders, with Eric's initiative and recommendation, had wisely begun getting John to help our congregation and community with its mental and emotional health. John had some great lines that stuck with me like this one: "Every morning we wake up and believe 'I am God's' OR 'I am God.'" It all depended on the apostrophe and the "s." I was amazed at some of the personal things John shared with us. I knew we must be in deep water. He did challenge Tracey and me to trust each other, but IVF made that so hard. I wasn't trusting that Trace would be ok if I had to say, "No more." Trace wasn't trusting that I would stick around and keep dealing with her grief.

John had a great illustration for us to consider. He drew a diagram of four balloons representing:

1. Core beliefs
2. Emotions
3. Thinking
4. Behaviors

These were all connected by straws and air could pass freely from one to another. Under peaceful circumstances, all the balloons were equal in size but under stress, air in the balloons would shift causing some to get bigger and some to get smaller. He talked about how Tracey's feeling balloon and my thinking balloon got too big under stress. We worked on ways to bring our internal systems back to equilibrium so that we could safely talk about our difficult issues. Ultimately, I was open to one more attempt if Tracey would take some time with God to process everything she was thinking and feeling. After my trip to Haiti in May, she would get away for a few days at a retreat center and wrestle with God. I praise God that Tracey and I were willing to go talk with John. I'm certain God used him to comfort us and save our marriage.

Reflect

- *What have been some difficult times in your marriage or another important relationship? What, if any, barriers do you feel about going to counseling?*

- ***Resource***: *The Meaning of Marriage by Tim and Kathy Keller*

29

Angry at IHOP

"This service that you perform is not only supplying the needs of the Lord's people but is also overflowing in many expressions of thanks to God."
2 Corinthians 9:12

My former apprentice, Micah, was now at Western Kentucky University. Micah and some of his students sold t-shirts and donated the profits to our Haiti trip. They raised $1,500! We were overwhelmed at the kingdom partnership and in awe of God's blessing on all our preparations. Everything had fallen into place since Milton's visit the previous fall. Milton met us in Haiti in May 2011; we took about 10 students. He gave us a great spiritual lens through which to see the trip with this verse: *"He defended the cause of the poor and needy and so all went well. Is that not what it means to know me? declares the Lord." Jeremiah 22:16*

Here I have smoothed out my journal reflections to give you a glimpse into the trip.

Family: *It was tough to leave Tracey and Miles behind. Reminded me that sometimes the gospel is more important than family. While missing my family back home, God was providing me new family in Haiti.*

- *Moise, the principal of the school, preacher for the church, and all-around handyman. He was my new dad in the faith.*
- *Youveline, the child we had started sponsoring the previous October. It was an amazing feeling to meet her and take pictures with her. She was my daughter in the faith.*
- *Our whole team fell in love with the hundreds of children in the school.*

Purpose: *I had that great feeling of "this is what I'm supposed to be doing." I got the feeling after checking on students before going to bed. I was reminded that I am responsible for them. I am a shepherd of their souls. But it's also wrapped up in service and mission as well. I want to shepherd college students while leading them into the mission of God.*

Service: *Our big project was clean water for the school. Our water team provided clean water for 250 kids and more because they shared it with families in the surrounding neighborhood.*

We had come to fix things but realized there was so much pain and need and love. We had a tremendously humbling experience at the "old folks' home." We rubbed lotion on the elderly—legs, hands, and feet. I led a few songs. One woman stood up with her walker. I thought she was trying to leave but instead, she started swaying to the music. She was dancing for God!

Incompetence: *I was up half the night with stomach trouble (which is common on your first trip to Haiti) and then taught a Bible class on worry from Matthew 6. I was very weak. We had studied the sermon on the mount in the spring semester so I thought it would be a good idea to take a direct approach and help the Haitians with their worry. There were lots of questions that Moise translated: "Is worry a sin?" "Does worry lead to sin?" "I haven't eaten yesterday or today but I focus on God and pray to him." "What do I do?" "If I worry, does that mean I did something wrong?" I was not prepared for this. My intentions were good, but later I wondered what a rich American Christian was doing trying to talk about worry. I wasn't rich by American standards, but I was compared to the rest of the world. I realized how insulated I was from some of the common worries of the world.*

I wrote this on Facebook the night we finished our work in Haiti: *"It's a great feeling to be worn out for God! Even when I am physically empty, I am spiritually full. I'm so proud of our team for their endurance and hard work and joy in the midst of so much struggle. When we left Haiti, one kid in the grass stuck both his arms in the air and waved with joy as we sped down the runway. I took it as a sign of hope and a reminder to come back."*

When I got home, I had what is called "reverse culture shock." The first day was a wonderful reunion with my family, but my second full day back in Oxford I was struggling with feeling emotionally numb. Since we were only in Haiti for eight days, I didn't have time to experience much culture shock there, so it happened when I got home and compared Haitian life to my own. I was angry at my American culture, especially the abundance and excess. I remember going to lunch with my family at IHOP and getting mad about the wasted food at other tables. It took me some time to remember that my American neighbors had not experienced what I had, and I needed a gracious approach to opening their eyes. One of the major ways I did this was by preaching and reporting on the trip to our church family. They had invested a lot financially and it was great to report back to them all the ways God had worked. It was encouraging to them and good therapy for me. As Paul had told us in 2 Corinthians, we were supplying the needs of the Lord's people in Haiti while many expressions of thanks to God were beginning to overflow in Haiti and Oxford.

Reflect

- *What do you think of short-term missions and why? Have you had any culture shock or reverse culture shock? Explain.*

30

Tracey's Shack

"We commend ourselves in every way; in great endurance; in troubles, hardships and distresses…" 2 Corinthians 6:4

Soon after I got settled from the trip to Haiti, Tracey left for her time of solitude. She would stay at a Catholic retreat center and hang out with a couple of nuns named Sister Clare and Sister Mary. Most of the time was spent in silence but you could talk at mealtimes. I told Miles that mama was going to have a special time with God. I was hoping and praying God would meet her there like he had met Mack in *The Shack*. I had no idea how life-changing those 3 days would be for her. She wrote about it in her journal and later posted it on her blog. Here are her words:

"Last summer (June 2011) I drove about two hours from home to a place of solitude. I needed solitude. Everyone does, and no one really has to go anywhere special for it, but I had felt a strong pull toward truly getting away to be with God for some time. I found a wonderful little place where I had a tiny cottage for two nights, and Casey's full support made it possible for me to have this time away guilt-free.

"While there, I spoke about twice each day with the lady who essentially ran the place. Clare is her name. I told her my very long story, going back to when Miles was born and getting to the place of grief I was currently in, the place where our dreams of more children had not been realized. I had been journaling during my solitude, and on the second day Clare suggested I write a letter in my journal to the children who had never come to be. I knew instantly that I didn't want to do that, and so it meant to me that I needed to do that. But it was going to be one of the hardest things I would write.

"It just so happened that Casey and I, over the course of our four failed in vitro cycles, had each come up with a name we liked if we ever had a boy or a girl. He had a girl's name in mind, I had decided on a boy's name. We had talked about them through each cycle, dreaming that one or both of them might be ours one day. The names had come to mean so much that I decided to address my letter to these two specific children.

***

"Dear Maggie and Moses,

I find it so very difficult to begin this letter. I fear that I will cling to the hope of you even more, and that hope has been discarded and trampled over and over again for more than three years.

Instead of sitting here writing a letter to children who don't exist, I should be holding you in my arms. I should be listening to your laughter as your big brother Miles is his usual, funny self. I thought that one or both of you might be here by now. None of that has come about as I dreamed...it's only been one more heartache after another.

How do I miss a child that never was? But I do — have seen you in my dreams, have imagined you coming home, have wondered what you would look like.

For so long, it has felt as if you were waiting for me at the end of this long journey; it was like I could see you as that light at the end of a torturous tunnel.

But now...now something I was sure would happen in time might never happen at all. Will I never know you? I struggle mightily to let you go.

If you are not to be, I need God to change the desires of my heart, because I cannot do it myself. This longing seems almost more than I can bear at times.

But oh, how you would be loved! And every day that you are not a reality makes me want to hold Miles that much closer. As much as I hope for you...well, he is here and you are not. God gave me such an amazing, beautiful boy in Miles Kendrick. I am desperate for him not to suffer because of my grief. He is loved, he is precious, he is pure — HE IS HERE. My love and delight need to be reserved for him, and not for a child that isn't.

I'm sorry, Maggie and Moses. Please come if you can. But if you can't, God will take care of us. I hate to say goodbye to you, but I need to lay the dream of you at Jesus' feet. He will know what to do.

I still want you...I do. But if my holding to the idea of you is futile, I am only doing a disservice to Casey and Miles. They need me, my heart, and my nurturing. They are my boys.

If you come someday, you will know what I mean. The love you will find in our little family is precious. It is waiting here if God's will is for you to be.
Love forever,
Mama"

Now you know why I had to include it because it is the most painfully beautiful thing in this book. God did what only God could do—he helped Tracey let go, to surrender, to lay the dream at Jesus' feet. My heart melted reading these words that were such a profound mix of surrender and sorrow that produced such joy in me. Later I would realize the power of spiritual direction that the nuns had used to help Tracey get to this point of writing such a powerful letter.

Reflect

- *What is something you've had to surrender or still need to surrender?*

- ***Resources:*** *Invitation to Solitude and Silence by Ruth Haley Barton*

- ***Respond:*** *Take 2-3 days for a quiet retreat and see how God meets you there.*

31

Church Politics 201—Mediator

Churches are notoriously slow to change. If you think our American government is slow to change after almost 250 years, imagine what it's like for the church which has been around for almost 2,000 years. This is good for many reasons. But a church with a campus ministry (or a youth ministry) is in a unique position. A campus ministry allows a slow-changing church to see what's coming around the corner faster because they are engaged with the next generation. The church gets to see what is important to students and wrestles with the needs of the local church versus the needs of the college students they are trying to reach. On the other hand, it can be frustrating for students because they only have 2-4 years with a church before they usually move on. They may help a church recognize a need or a problem, but sometimes it only gets addressed or resolved after they leave. Sometimes once those students leave, the issue gets dropped to avoid a conflict with the local church.

We had a moment in 2011 when the tension between church and campus came to a head. It was over public expressions of worship—things like clapping, lifting hands, singing more contemporary songs. (Note: Some of you will understand this situation well while others of you may be perplexed that we had to deal with this, but this was our mission context, and I know you understand it is hard to go against the long-standing traditions of your church or ministry.) Megan (some called her "Soup" because her last name was Campbell and it stuck) was a student who found her way into our ministry because of Nick, one of our interns. She started with the campus ministry but slowly started coming to worship with us on Sundays as well. It's also important to note she came from a different church background, so she came with different experiences and ideas about worship. It was my job to mediate and bridge the gap between our church and campus, so I connected these students to our church leadership. Here's what I wrote after that meeting:

"Had a watershed moment in our leadership meeting last night. Soup came and shared her heart about worship. There were a lot of powerful moments.

1. *Soup mentioned the Luke 19 verse about the rocks crying out. I had never thought of that verse in the context of worship before but wow, what a great application.*
2. *Soup said old vs. new is not the problem. We just need more songs that let us rejoice.*
3. *Worship is not about comfort but those who want to express joy in worship should feel like they can do that.*
4. *I felt the struggle to talk about heart vs. externals. What does joy look like?*
5. *The most profound testimony was Soup sharing that worship is not about what I get out of it. It's about God. She talked about how God tore her down this year learning that about worship.*

    Thank you, Lord, for Soup. Please let the ripple effects begin by the power of your Spirit."

I was so proud of Soup for sharing her heart and the way she did it—a great combination of passion and thought. For a young adult to see that worship is ultimately not about what we get out of it is huge. Two months later, our leadership had an important meeting about the issue.

"Last night was important for RFC and the church. We met to discuss joyful worship as a case study. I had fasted on Monday in preparation for this. The meeting ended up being a Spirit-driven blessing! The conversations went well—a little intense but generally healthy. By the end, I was blown away that one elder was proposing a permission-giving announcement to the church that some joyful expression was ok. It's probably not wise to make a general announcement right now but the spirit of his words was a 180-degree turn. I got to share with Soup afterward and she was encouraged."

I affirm our elders for ultimately being willing to have the conversation. Just to hear students out is a big win though you have to help students understand that it is a win. You might wonder why we didn't just send out that permission-giving announcement. It's complicated, but the elders needed more time to figure out exactly how they wanted to proceed with both church and students. It is always hard to juggle the needs of church members with that of students. I know the atmosphere became more joyful over time and that was a big win—helping a reverent, subdued church family come to see that the Spirit was trying to use students' passion for Jesus to give them more joy in worship.

Again, if your ministry is not connected to a local church this might not even be an issue. You might think the disconnect is a blessing and it can be in the short term. But in the long term, we have to remember that our campus ministries are NOT the church and that someday soon, graduating students will have to find their way into local churches. So, let's help prepare them any way we can.

I'm sure your situation will be different in some details. Maybe your church or campus ministry is past these struggles over worship but I'm sure there is an issue that brings tension with it. This is a great case study in how God may call us to mediate and bridge the gap between church and campus, having old and new generations listen to one another and grappling with tradition, culture and the Bible. To have church elders and students in the same room listening to one another and wrestling with an issue is a huge win. As Jesus suggested in Matthew 13:52, how do we, as disciples bring out of our storeroom new treasures as well as old?

Reflect

- *What is a similar experience you've had with worship or another issue of tension between two groups?*

32

Creating a Landmine

If I did some digging, I know I could remember more, but the only thing I really remember about our 2011 conference was that Shane Claiborne spoke. He did almost all the keynote talks based on his book *The Irresistible Revolution*.[41] Shane had done some amazing things like visit Iraq and meet Mother Teresa. He was someone I could imagine being a modern-day Jesus, getting into good trouble. He had a lot of quotable lines:

1. We don't accept Jesus through force, but fascination, not taught but caught
2. Our deepest passion connects with our deepest pain
3. Loving people back to God
4. None above reproach, none beyond redemption

He talked about Saul (who became Paul) as a terrorist. I had never thought about Saul like that. He told radical stories of love and forgiveness.

-   A family did not seek the death penalty against a man who killed their child. The man became a Christian.

-   There was a well-known story of how the Amish forgave the shooter in Pennsylvania. They went to be with his family and gave scholarships to his kids.

-   A robotics engineer created a robot that would dismantle landmines, so kids didn't have to do it.

---

[41] Shane Claiborne, *The Irresistible Revolution: 10th Anniversary Edition*, Grand Rapids: Zondervan, 2016.

- A Harvard lawyer worked pro bono in Alabama (I believe this was Bryan Stephenson).

This is a short chapter but it's important for two reasons. First, Shane was someone I took seriously as a follower of Jesus. He was radical to some, but he was gentle, humble, and thoughtful. He had learned, as Camp suggested in *Mere Discipleship*, many of the implications of Jesus being Lord. I felt like I knew his heart well after reading his book and hearing him speak several times. Second, I used some of his thoughts and stories in my lessons over the next several years and most of the time, it went over well. But little did I know, as I was drawn to Jesus through Shane's faith, I was unintentionally creating a landmine that I would step on in a sermon almost six years later.

Reflect

- *What story of Shane's impressed you the most? What's a book you loved that also challenged you?*

33

The Future of Our Family

*"So then, death is at work in us, but life is
at work in you." 2 Corinthians 4:12*

After four failed IVF attempts, marriage at its breaking point, and God intervening at a retreat center in the middle of nowhere Mississippi, we were ready to try one last time. The complication this time was that we would have to use donor eggs. Our doctor told us that, unfortunately, after everything Tracey had been through, her eggs were not healthy enough for fertilization. Our families rallied around us and helped us raise the money needed to try this last time. I hope you can hear the desperation in my journal as 2012 began:

> *"O God, the end of IVF is near. The beginning of new life or more grief is near. The embryo transfer is next Tuesday. The pregnancy test is Thursday, January 19th. I am at peace in many ways. But I need this time with you far from the tempest and storm. (Psalm 55). Come and right these wrongs of barrenness and infertility. Open Tracey's womb like the women of old you used to help in their desperation."*

We were desperate...like many people who came to Jesus. As it happened, one of our favorite teachers and speakers, Randy Harris, was speaking at Gulf Coast Getaway (GCG)—a large student conference we went to every year. We knew we wanted to ask him to pray for us. Though we had a relationship with God, there was something about Randy and his relationship with God that attracted us to him. It makes me think of the woman who touched Jesus thinking, "If I just touch his clothes, I will be healed."[42] Randy seemed to us like the clothing of Jesus. We asked and he agreed to pray for us. Here was a man of faith praying on behalf of us in our feeble faith. We were like the dad who confessed his feeble faith, "I do believe. Help me overcome my unbelief."[43]

On January 19th, Tracey took the test and we waited…all day. She knitted, I painted. By 5 pm we had given up hope of hearing anything that day. But at supper, God used Eric to call and give us the news—Tracey was pregnant! And the Beta number was high enough that it could be twins. We were stunned and joyful. Soon after this, an ultrasound would confirm two sacks and two heartbeats visibly fluttering. After 15,000 miles of travel between Oxford and Birmingham over five IVF cycles, God had granted us the desires of our hearts.

In a few more weeks we would learn we were having a boy and a girl. We would be having the Maggie and Moses Tracey had written to a year earlier. Tracey made it 37 weeks but on September 5, it was time for the twins to enter the world. The picture I took showing them resting beautifully on their mother is forever etched in my memory. Tracey could not have looked prouder or happier. We even skyped into the Wednesday night Bible class to show off our family to students. In 2006, we were home after roughly 100 days in the hospital. This time we were coming home after 2 days. Over six years to get the redemption we had longed for!

However, the fall semester was rough for both the family and the ministry. Familywise, I couldn't really complain after what Tracey had gone through, but I did get shingles, a weird eye disease, ringworm, and my first ever cavity because I was falling apart from the lack of sleep. Ministry-wise, I was barely treading water and sometimes drowning. Upperclassmen were supportive and helpful, but as is always the case with the turnover in campus ministry, there were freshmen who had no idea what we had been through and it was probably not the best experience for them. This was one of those times that family would get more attention than ministry. Just like we did for Miles and Brian (Eric and Melanie's son), we planted trees for Maggie and Moses. A magnolia tree for Maggie because we decided to make her name short for Magnolia. For Moses, we planted a maple tree just like Brian's. We taught Moses that Brian was like a second older brother.

---

42 Mark 5:28
43 Mark 9:24

As you can imagine, those early months were both wonderful and hard. Paul was right—death was at work in us parents, but life was at work in the twins. It was over a year before the twins would sleep through the night. I battled the haze of sleepiness and temptation during the day and night. I was spiritually weak. It was hard to find God in my sleepy stupor just trying to survive another day. It was yet another time I felt incompetent at managing my life, family and ministry.

Reflect

- *Reflect on my journal entries below. What do you think about parenting as discipleship?*

- ***March 2014:*** *"Thank you for these precious gifts you give us for just a few years. They are your gifts to us and our gifts to the world."*

- ***May 2014:*** *"More than anything we long to see our kids find Jesus to be for themselves everything we said he was and more. Lord, help Miles, Maggie and Moses come to know you personally."*

Section 3:

The Competent Years

34

A Verse for the Incompetent

It was hard to know where to put "The Competent Years" in my story. Often when I felt competent in ministry, I felt incompetent in my family and vice versa. Maybe God does that on purpose. While Tracey was flying to Austin, Texas, with Miles for her *double* baby shower, I was headed back to Haiti for year two. Everything was going so well. Our church was supportive, financially and spiritually. I was able to be part of the mission I loved taking students to Haiti. And Tracey was glowing as her body was now growing the two children we had fought so hard to bring into this world with God's mighty help. So, I felt competent in my family life by God's grace. But a third-world mission trip has a way of revealing more incompetence. I journaled some of the ways.

Fear: *"We hit some mild turbulence and I became pretty anxious and afraid. My fear of flying became my fear of dying, which became my fear of leaving all my family behind and I cried and teared up for several minutes. I heard Jesus' words, 'Why are you so afraid?' I looked over and saw Milton sleeping. That's what I wanted."*

Discomfort: *"After the comfort of sleeping at a resort in our first year, we stayed at the Cap Haitien Children's Home in the heat with our portable fans. We used mosquito nets. I had trouble sleeping and every day felt tired. This was certainly a more realistic picture of how the Haitians lived; except they didn't have nets. I read Psalm 139:8 one evening—' If I go up to the heavens, you are there. If I make my bed in the depths, you are there.' It made me think of Oxford and Haiti. Oxford felt like the heavens and Haiti like the depths. God is wherever I go. I cannot escape his presence…which is great news. God is here in Haiti. We've been saying it and now I must believe it."*

Unknown: *"The morning we left for Benjamin (a village hours away from the city), I read the verse from Isaiah that would change my life. 'I will lead the blind by ways they have not known; along unfamiliar paths I will guide them. I will turn their darkness into light before them and make the rough places smooth. These are the things I will do. I will not forsake them.*[44] *Our team traveled in the open air of a covered truck. The scenery was epic as we traveled up and over a mountain. Travel was terribly bumpy as the roads had potholes that felt like we were going through the Grand Canyon every quarter mile. We passed through at least one major river…literally. As we approached Benjamin, it truly felt like the middle of nowhere. We walked down to a different river where 20 Haitians were baptized. We had an amazing dinner with Alfred (the CRF Director) and his family. We learned the next day that we had slept in their beds while they slept in a shed nearby."*

Generosity: *"James (co-leader with Milton) shared that they first came to Alfred 18 years ago. They couldn't drive the whole way without using machetes to provide enough clearing for the truck to pass. He was impressed with Alfred. He didn't ask for things, he said 'Come and see.' James got choked up sharing how Alfred's family gave a chicken, five mangoes, and a dozen eggs as a thank-you gift when he knew they didn't have enough to share. I couldn't help but think of this verse that only now made sense: 'In the midst of a very severe trial, their overflowing joy and their extreme poverty welled up in rich generosity. For I testify that they gave as much as they were able, and even beyond their ability."*[45]

Fear, discomfort, the unknown and experiencing a generosity that put my giving to shame—all these contributed to my incompetence and yet as Isaiah had promised, God had not forsaken me or our team. The blindness described in Isaiah is a perfect metaphor for incompetence because none of us really knows where our lives are headed. But God was obviously leading the way and using others more competent than me as guides—like Milton, James, and Alfred. Over time, whether on a mission trip or in life, he turns our darkness into light and makes us competent.

After the trip, I shared again with the Oxford church. Thirty more children were sponsored!

In case you got lost in the Haiti details, let me summarize what was so important about this experience.

- We were partnering with the Christian Relief Fund (CRF) because we had hosted the conference and invited Milton to speak.

---

[44] Isaiah 42:16
[45] 2 Corinthians 8:2-3

- We were giving about ten college students each year a chance to experience third-world missions. I consider that a tremendous investment in discipleship.

- The church was graciously on board, supporting our team with generous donations and sponsoring Haitian children. Only God could produce this kind of synergy and partnership between the church and campus—a huge blessing for my ministry. And again, it was fueled by a larger kingdom purpose: caring for the people of Haiti.

After a few more years, we would be sponsoring about 100 children because of our mission trips. This monthly, regular investment in the children of Haiti is what could produce long-term change in a very broken country. I didn't know it would be my last trip for the foreseeable future, but in 2018, we took a Let's Start Talking (LST) team to help Haitians with their English using the Bible. I was thankful for how far God had brought us since 2011. For eight years, God had led us (the blind) by exciting and trying ways we had never known, along unfamiliar paths. Darkness was turned into light and the rough places were made smooth for both the Americans and the Haitians.

Reflect

- *How does the Isaiah verse make sense of your own personal or missional experiences?*

35

Learning to Love Greeks

"Be wise in the way you act toward outsiders. Make the most of every opportunity." Colossians 4:3,5

I have come a long way from my early days in campus ministry. Even with the name change, AΩ Christian Student Center, I had, at best, tried to ignore Greek life at Ole Miss which had created a sense of isolation and an "us versus them" mentality. At worst, I resented these fraternities and sororities for taking students from me so I could not build a bigger ministry. God forgive me. Even as late as 2014, I still struggled with feeling like I had to compete with Greek life, and when it feels like a competition, you've already lost.

September 14, 2014: *"The Feast of a Thousand Chickens is tonight. Excited some but sad/angry as well. RUSH started today (Greek recruitment period) so some of our students will be missing in action. God, it's so hard to compete with everything. God, help us to reach all we can reach. Help us to be content with who you give but also discontent and reach out to those who weren't invited."*

It was so hard to find the perfect date for our events and there always seemed to be a conflict coming from some direction. I'm sure this is part of why I grew weary of events. I didn't want to put this journal quote in, but I wanted you to know the struggle was real. Every time I was disappointed, I had to give it to God and learn to let go and focus on those who did come. Every minister understands this. There's often another youth group or a different church that we feel like we have to compete with. I hope this chapter prepares you to face the spirit of competition that is common in ministry.

As I matured and God softened my heart, he helped me to love Greek students where they were. I gave up trying to force them to be leaders in RFC or even regular participants. I learned Greek life was demanding and took up most of their time outside of class. If a Greek student came to Sunday worship or Wednesday night class, that was a win. Still, I wanted to engage with them. With CRF in my mission's toolbox, I connected with Kelsey, a Greek student who came to worship most Sundays. I knew each sorority or fraternity had a philanthropy that they raised money for each year. Some had multiple good causes they were already supporting, but I wondered if some of them might still be looking for a great cause. I asked Kelsey if the ladies at AOII would want to make a difference in the lives of young women who can't go to school because they have to fetch water daily. Kelsey wrote this in September 2013 and it forever changed the way I viewed Christian students in Greek life: *"One of my major convictions is to be active in the mission field God places you in, and one of those for me happens to be the Greek system. I'll most definitely be there next Wednesday and try to bring a bunch of other AOIIs with me! Last week and this week have been crazy with rush! I'm so glad AOII was able to pick them (CRF) up as a philanthropy!*

Kelsey connected me with the President of AOII, Kelly, and I explained the vision to her. On September 10, 2013, I wrote, *"Today I spoke with Kelly. They want to send CRF $5,000 to dig a well in Kenya. Praise God and make it so!"* I could not believe how easily that had happened. I had been looking for a fraternity as well and somehow God connected me with William and the Phi Delts. They raised money for a well too. I still have the picture CRF took of the wells when they were finished, and a plaque placed by the well to thank those who had given. Somewhere in the African desert, people are drinking water because God had softened my heart to Greek students, and they responded with tremendous generosity.[46]

This chapter is a great contrast to the coffee house chapter. Paul and Colossians had given me this great open-door theology for making the most of my opportunities. And it was practically working! God had taught me to love Greek students and partner with them for a greater kingdom cause. As the years went on, more Christian Greek students felt safe at RFC and engaged with us more often than once a week. They would bring their Greek friends. Sometimes they would choose an RFC event over a Greek event. But

---

[46] Milton wrote a touching tribute based on a lot of work done in 2013. (From Milton Jones blog: https://blog.christianrelieffund.org/be-like-casey/)

thankfully I was past the competition and keeping score. God had changed my heart and I just wanted them to know the love of Jesus in whatever time I had with them.

Reflect

- *What is your relationship with Greek life like? (or any group you feel threatened by) What positive or negative perceptions do you bring to the relationship?*

36

Presidential Ministry

June 2012: *"Delaware sounds great to me. Great opportunity to remember the great need in the Northeast like Jason Locke reminded us of in 2004. Delaware could be a flagship campus ministry for future ministry in the Northeast."*

A s you can see, I wrote this in the summer of 2012 as we were considering the location of our 2013 conference where Tyler Ellis was campus minister. Delaware was a good trigger for me to remember my first conference in 2004 at West Virginia and the vision Jason had cast. I was honored to become a board member soon after I had hosted the 2010 conference. The Board did vote to allow Delaware to host the 2013 conference and we met on the University of Delaware's campus in August. Trent Sheppard was our speaker. His book, *God on Campus* has some great stories of how God worked on campus, especially in the Northeast, but it's also a great reminder for any ministry of why we should pray and how prayer changes things and brings revival.

I remember it being a small group that made the trip to Delaware, but it was still special. My apprentice, Deonte, came with me, and I was glad we could give him this experience to see the larger network of campus ministers. At our board meeting, after the conference, I was voted in as the new President of the Campus for Christ Board which was also a new name for our organization. Jim Barnett was the previous President and wrote this to the existing Board members calling for a vote before the conference:

"I have spoken with Casey, and he is willing to take this (the presidency) on now. Therefore, I would like to nominate Casey to be the President of the

Board of the organization…Campus for Christ. I do this based on the following points:

- Casey is a man of integrity with a heart for college campuses nationwide. Not only does he have a vibrant ministry at Ole Miss, but he has also been active in trying to recruit and train leaders who will go into campus ministry.

- He has been a campus minister for numerous years and is well-respected among our peers.

- He works at a conservative church, but he has also shown a propensity to be open-minded and willing to push the envelope if unity will not be threatened.

- I believe Casey is the type of leader who will work to find consensus among our Board and the decisions we make, but I also believe him to be capable and willing to decide on his own if time is of the essence, and I trust him enough to know that he will be able to defend his decision, with one reason being he believed it was in the best interest of the group.

- Finally, I like him and believe that all of you do too.

I was honored that Jim and the Board were supportive of me. Their support was a beautiful affirmation of the calling God had given me to be in campus ministry. Looking back, it is terribly humbling to be honored in this way and I have peace knowing it was not something I sought. It was a blessing to see how God had taken my competence (and incompetence) with training apprentices, hosting a conference, and being a team player to honor me with the title of "President" for the organization I loved. This honor was yet another this-is-what-I'm-supposed-to-be-doing moment. God was turning all those years of incompetence into competence.

Reflect

- *What is one of your this-is-what-I'm-supposed-to-be-doing moments?*

- **Resource**: *God on Campus by Trent Sheppard*

37

Sharpen the Axe

"No discipline seems pleasant at the time but painful. Later on, however, it produces a harvest of righteousness and peace for those who have been trained by it." Hebrews 12:11

February 2012: *"I think we all long for this personal conversation with God but we don't know how to position ourselves to hear him. I think God reveals himself more in quiet ways. The world shouts to get our attention. God quietly waits for the world to quiet down or for us to withdraw from it."*

This is one of my favorite parables that I come back to often.

Once upon a time, there were two woodcutters named Peter and John. One day, they decided to hold a competition to determine who was the best. The rules were simple—whoever produced the most wood in a day would win. So, the next day morning, both of them took up their positions in the forest and started chopping away in their fastest possible speed. This lasted for an hour before Peter suddenly stopped. When John realized that there was no chopping sound from his opponent's side, he thought: "Ah Ha! He must be tired already!" And he continued to cut down his trees with double the pace. A quarter of an hour passed, and John heard his opponent chopping again. John was starting to feel weary when the chopping from Peter stopped once again. Feeling motivated and smelling victory close by, John continued, with a smile on his face. This went on the whole day. Every hour, Peter would stop chopping for fifteen minutes while John kept going relentlessly. When the competition ended, John was absolutely confident that he would take the triumph. But to John's astonishment, Peter had actually cut down more wood. How did this even happen? "How could you have chopped down more trees than me? I heard you stop working every hour for fifteen minutes!", *exclaimed John. Peter replied, "Well, it's really simple. While you kept going, I* *was sharpening my axe."*[47]

Early in my ministry, I remember getting in the habit of coming into my office, immediately opening my computer, and beginning to answer emails, send texts, plan events, craft lessons, and more—all good, important work. And yet, it was starting to stress me out. My chest started to tighten; my face got all tingly. I was unsettled. I didn't look forward to going to my office. I don't know how much of it was just normal human reactions to the responsibilities of life or whether it had something to do with how I was wired.

I remember having a desk for the kind of work I described…a really grand dark wood desk that seemed fit more for a preacher than a campus minister. Over by the window in my office, I decided to set up a folding table and put several of my best devotional books on it. This would be the table where I developed my spiritual roots. At one point, I was reading the Psalms. I wrote this on **November 1, 2011:** *"Just read Psalm 55. Verses 6-8 stood out to me: 'Oh, that I had the wings of a dove! I would fly away and be at rest. I would flee far away and stay in the desert; I would hurry to my place of shelter, far from the tempest and storm.' What a description of solitude! I want to become the kind of disciple who hurries to my shelter. O God, make it so!"*

These verses changed my life. There was a period of 5-7 years where I said those words almost every day to start my quiet time with God and I still say them regularly over ten years later. God used those words like a portal to transport me to another world—to fly away from my burdensome work to the world where I tended to my relationship with God and just got to be with him and rest. This place was far away from the tempest and storm of public ministry. Early on all it took was being at a different desk in my office to find that rest. I can see how this can sound like an escape from life, and I suppose it's possible to abuse such time. But 30 minutes (or even an hour) of quiet time compared to 8-10 hours of ministry work in a day should not feel like an escape but an essential component of ministry. After all, Luke 5:16 tells us, *"Jesus often withdrew to lonely places and prayed."* There were sometimes in 2011 when I was desperate for solitude and I referenced Henri Nouwen's book *The Way of the Heart.* It is a must-read for every minister.

---

[47] https://screeble.com/blog/2017/03/07/story-of-two-woodcutters/

October 25, 2011: *"Needing solitude, the desert is the place of salvation. Nouwen is right. I am a compulsive minister. Too easily am I swayed by circumstances. I have been angry at students. Nouwen says solitude is the furnace of transformation. We must face our anger and greed in solitude. Even coming to work this morning, I feel the desire to be compulsive, to get to work, be busy, and do. O God teach me not to be compulsive."*

October 30: *"O God, I am frustrated because many things bother me right now. I have seen my ministry be a blessing and effective by most standards and yet I am not happier but more frustrated. I need solitude. I have come to see it today as friendship with God. It shows that we are friends because I spend time with you. Not only do I want this time, I need this time. I see how easily I would rather work and get things done than to stop and be quiet with you—the one I should want to be with. O God turn my heart towards you so I don't become an enemy to you, myself, or others."*

You will notice I discovered Psalm 55 two days after this last journal entry. God was at work! I am so glad I recognized my need for time with God and fought against the need to be productive. *I discovered that solitude was sharpening my axe.* But after a while, my soul was telling me I needed to get out of the office. Now I knew how Jesus felt when he wanted to get away. About this same time, my shepherd, Eric, was talking to me about the benefits of exercise. He mentioned how walking got the blood flowing to every blood vessel in the body for 11 minutes. He said there was another health benefit at 20 minutes and then another boost at 30 minutes. There was the beautiful Lamar Park on the way to the office with a winding walk track and a pond, so I started there. I set a timer for 11 minutes, walked and talked with God, got back in the car, and headed to work. I did my 11 minutes for weeks. I developed a hunger for it and sensed I was ready for 20 minutes. I set a timer, walked and talked with God, then headed off to work. Somewhere during this time, a thought occurred to me on the really cold days—I could wear my big deer hunting jacket, put on my gloves, and sometimes even a sock hat to protect my ears. So, I got all bundled up and headed out for 20 minutes. I was proud that I had found a way to still get out there on a cold day. Then another thought occurred to me on rainy days—I could buy a big umbrella. Just that small investment allowed me to get out in all kinds of weather. It was during these walks that I started every walk with the words of Psalm 55:6-8. I would be freezing, but exhilarated, as I began walking with the words, *"I would flee far away and stay in the desert."* Lamar Park certainly didn't look like a desert, but it functioned like one. My shoes would be soaking wet at the end of my rainy walks, but my heart was full of gratitude that I had been with God "far from the tempest and storm." Sometimes I would prayer walk in an actual storm, but it was still the most special time I had with God that day.

As I got up to 30 minutes regularly, I memorized passages of Scripture. I slowly added 10-15 texts like the Lord's Prayer, the Philippian and Colossian hymns, Psalm 23, parts of Hebrews 12, 2 Corinthians 4, and one of my favorites, Romans 12:9-21 which I still recite almost every Wednesday. I hesitate to tell you all this, but I want you to know how special this time was to me and how the Holy Spirit helped me grow deeper with God. I would recite a passage or two and then pray about my family. I would walk quietly for a while and then pray another passage. I would pray for particular students, lessons I would be working on that day, and meetings I would be having. I was learning to cover everything in prayer, and it was awesome. Prayer walking had become a new way for me to sharpen my axe. Little did I realize in the early days of this new spiritual discipline that God was preparing me for some new challenges that were on the horizon. Some were exciting but some were going to test me like never before. Sometimes you can run from the storm, but sometimes, all you can do is prepare for it.

Reflect

- *What is your desire for solitude with God. How hard is it to pursue? What's one small step you can take toward solitude with God in your daily life?*

- **Resource**: *The Way of the Heart by Henri Nouwen*

38

Family or Ministry?

"For we are taking pains to do what is right, not only in the eyes of the Lord but also in the eyes of man." 2 Corinthians 8:21

Looking back, I should have stayed home in 2013 when the twins were eight months old and not gone to Haiti. Hindsight, am I right? But when we had another good group ready for 2015, I sensed it was time to take a break, honor my wife, and stay home. I had led a team for four straight years and things were going so well. I felt the team would be fine with some returning students assisting our new students. Milton was planning to go and meet the team there. All I needed now was a team leader from Oxford. Thankfully, a church member, Jonathan, stepped up to lead the team. He was a good friend and a little crazy so I knew the students would enjoy time with him. Sadly, while on the trip, Milton's mother passed away and he left as soon as he could to return home. I felt so bad for Milton and guilty that I had not gone. I felt somewhat responsible even though I had made as good a decision as I could at the time. Milton was gracious. Deep down we knew it was no one's fault, just bad timing.

The thing I did not anticipate was a church member coming to an elder's meeting sometime in the summer questioning me on why I didn't go on the trip. First of all, I had already gotten the elders' blessing to stay home. That should have been the end of it. If this person had a problem with the decision, it should have been taken to the elders, not me, in my opinion. Second of all, I wasn't sure why this was being brought before the entire eldership. It seemed like a meeting for me and this member to have on our own time with maybe one elder. I was hurt. Part of this shows my sensitivity. I wish I had just explained the situation as best I could without getting hurt and not thought about it anymore and had a great night's sleep. That didn't happen. In **July 2007**, I recorded this in my journal (different church member):

"Church member: How long have you been here?

Casey: Over three years

Church member: Don't you think it's about time you started doing something?

Casey to myself: It actually doesn't hurt like I thought it would. God is helping me to sift and sort and love and forget and forgive and even learn from well-intentioned brothers and sisters."

I'm not quite sure why the 2007 comment bounced off while the 2015 comment was absorbed and I allowed it to fester in my soul. I'm sure there were many variables. I believe the biggest had to do with the tension of family and ministry. There isn't a graduate class or spiritual book that prepares you for this tension and the tension is always there—every day. Granted the tension was magnified for me because of Tracey's health issues, IVF, and then having twins. There are plenty of days when ministry or family requires more of your time. There are many days where your family or ministry will be disappointed or frustrated with you, and it took me years to begin handling their disappointment in a healthy way. It takes wisdom to know who to pick and sometimes you can get it wrong.

I am the type of person who gets hurt when I feel like I'm doing the best I can, and it still doesn't seem to be good enough for someone. I am also the type of person who replays events over and over with what I said, what they said, and what I should have said. I have learned that I am an overthinker when I experience emotions that are hard for me to process. This gets back to my thinking balloon getting too big under stress. I defended my thought process the best I could—I stayed home to support Tracey, Jonathan stepped up, etc.—and left the meeting discouraged. I sent this to an elder sometime after the meeting: "I am totally ok wrestling with the best way to spend my time and sincerely want yours and Eric's guidance with that, but I hope it is clear that I am working for the kingdom." To my knowledge, the trip went well and there were no major issues among the team. I thought this would be a little sabbatical for me and a great chance to delegate and empower others on the team to step up (like my growth reviews had encouraged me to do). Unfortunately, it seemed to backfire.

We did, however, invite Moise to Oxford in September for our big student weekend with the church. It was so cool to bring this dear Haitian brother to Mississippi. We took him to a football game; he preached on Sunday morning and led a prayer Sunday night with 75+ students on stage behind him. That was a healing time. I don't think I'll ever be completely unaffected by complaints but I'm still learning to see them as part of God's training to keep me humble. If God opposes the proud but gives grace to the humble,[48] then I want to be humble (whether the complaint is valid or not) because I desperately need his grace.

Reflect

- *What would you have done in my situation about going to Haiti or staying home? How sensitive are you to the complaints of others?*

---

[48] 1 Peter 5:5

39

Fundraising for Jesus

"Each of you should give what you have decided in your heart to give, not
reluctantly or under compulsion, for God loves a cheerful giver."
2 Corinthians 9:7

After the 2013 Conference in Delaware, the host, Tyler Ellis, had
encouraged us to buy a book called *The God Ask* by Steve Shadrach. I
ordered it and didn't think much about it for a year. After the 2014
conference, something prompted me to remember the book. This time I
called Scott Lambert, a good friend and former campus minister, who had
raised support for his ministry. He talked about Support Raising Solutions as
the catalyst for his work. This was the organization behind the book that
regularly offered the boot camps. He called support raising "the bottleneck
issue" of our day. Why? Because too many ministry dreams have died because
there wasn't enough money. For a long time, our churches have been able to
support our ministry fully. But what if the church begins to decline? What if
you want to do something new or different…a new event, new facilities?
What if you want more staff? Train apprentices? What if you want to help
plant new ministries? You would run a very high risk of your proposal getting
shot down simply because of a lack of money. Scott also made an interesting
parallel—support raising similar to evangelism. I was scared and fascinated.
If I was willing to ask people to support my vision for ministry financially, it
took a similar courage to ask people to consider Jesus.

I remember a simple but profound train of thought occurred. I have
done ministry for 10 years. I knew alumni, friends, and family who would be

willing to support me. I knew I could find 10 people who would give $100/month. That's $12,000 a year. After reading the book, I knew I could find 20 people who would give $100/month, $24,000 a year. After doing the homework and attending the support raising boot camp, I knew I could find 30 people who would give $100/month, $36,000 a year. This was a game-changer.

I joked afterward that the boot camp was an introvert's nightmare. It was two long, draining days. But it had trained me in nearly every situation I would encounter in the coming months. At the boot camp, we prepared and practiced our presentation and learned how to respond to a "yes," "no," or "maybe." Early on it felt awkward and forced but similar to evangelism, the more I practiced, the more natural and organic it became. I created a presentation that told my story from Arkansas to ACU to Ole Miss. I talked in detail about the ministry at Ole Miss. Our vision was for *Rebels for Christ to be a training center to reach the nation and the nations*. This vision incorporated our apprenticeship and our outreach to American and International students. I wanted to raise my support to demonstrate to apprentices that I was not asking them to do something I had not done myself. This made it more authentic, and I knew it would help our relationship if I were in the trenches with them.

Once I got through the boot camp, the next big thing I had to do was get my elders on board. This paradigm of raising support was not normal for established campus ministries and had never been done at Ole Miss so I knew it would take some time for them to process my proposal, ask questions and hopefully get on board. I went individually to all six of my elders. One of the tricky parts was that I asked to receive 1/6th of the funds I raised. With all the medical bills over the years, our health insurance being high, and the fact that the worker was worth his wages, I believed it was a fair request. Thankfully, after a few short weeks (lightspeed in church time), God got us all going in the same direction and the elders were supportive and commissioned me to begin the task. Plus, Doug Sr. was eager to support my vision as an added bonus.

I shared with a few friends and family at Thanksgiving and Christmas. December and January were great months to work on this as the campus ministry load was light. It was intimidating to ask people to support my vision for RFC with their money, but I believed so strongly in the vision that I got over the fear. I tried to visit as many people face-to-face as possible, but there were a few I simply shared with over the phone. Here is one great example I journaled in December: *"Yesterday I shared my presentation with a friend over the phone. At the end, she responded that she was in for $100 a month. When I checked my email later, she had already donated. But it was $200 monthly. I got choked up. When I emailed her today, she talked about how excited she was to be part of this and how it gave her accounting job a greater purpose. I was humbled and honored."* This friend had proven 2 Corinthians 9 to be true. I had heard stories at the boot camp of people being excited to donate and honored that someone would ask. Though my family always had everything we needed, it was hard to donate extra for good causes. I realized there really were people out there who wanted to help with this kind of kingdom work.

After a good bit of initial success, some fears began to creep back in. I wrote this in February: *"Fears—people supporting the vision, raising enough money, keeping the support going, the vision becoming a reality, having enough candidates for the apprenticeship."* Some people said "no" or didn't respond to a text or an email. I would wait a week and try again. Paranoia started to creep in with thoughts in my head about how they were probably trying to ignore me as their way of saying "no." Most of the time, my text or email got lost in all the texts and emails, and at some point, we would connect and many said "yes." Some gave monthly while others gave annually.

After four-plus months of work, April 1st turned out to be an amazing day. "When I got home there was a piece of mail from a donor I had invited to join my support team. My pulse quickened. Inside was a check for $3,000. I was blown away. This came out of nowhere for me, but God had been at work. I had been at $33,000 in my support raising so that quickly took me to my goal of $36,000 annually. Scott said there would be some surprises, and he was right!" Scott had also said, "The longer we live, the more we learn to trust." I was proof of that. I had done something similar when leaving engineering. You wouldn't expect a careful, cautious, calculating man like me to do something like this, but God has a way of showing us a better way to live when our eyes are open. And when we trust God, we really can move mountains.

Reflect

- *How do you feel about raising money for your ministry and why?*

- **Resource:** *The God Ask by Steve Shadrach and the bootcamp website:* <ins>*https://www.vianations.org/generosity/trainings/via/bootcamp*</ins>

40

Coaching Apprentices

"Thanks be to God, who put it into the heart of Titus the same concern I have for you." 2 Corinthians 8:16

My dad and grandfather had been basketball coaches and now I was learning to coach too, but in a different way—making disciples. Coaching is hard work. There are varying degrees of joy and frustration with your players depending on their:

- Skillset (spiritual gifts and talents)
- Willingness to put in the work (he or she who hears and puts into practice)
- Previous training and experience (healthy habits, good or bad theology, etc.)

Then there were my limitations:

- Limited amount of time
- Learning to coach while coaching
- Care for my struggling family

You will recall that Lendy was my first apprentice, and he served with us three years before transitioning to our full-time preacher position. Still, we had a big vision for training others in campus ministry who would someday fill established ministry roles or start new ones as part of a campus ministry plant.

Micah (and his wife Katie) started working with us as an apprentice in 2009. Micah had come to Ole Miss to work on a philosophy degree. He had been in Jim Brinkerhoff's Auburn ministry. I had consulted with Jim a few times and his campus ministry was well known and highly respected in Churches of Christ. Micah was naturally brilliant and that made me a little insecure and intimidated by him. Laura was our female apprentice during this time as well. She was working on a master's degree and taught classes on campus. I believe she received awards for her teaching. So, I had two high-quality apprentices working with ME—a first-generation, kind-of equipped campus minister. Being in their presence increased my feelings of incompetence. Micah had great instincts because of his time at Auburn and he had good teaching skills and was great at strengthening our guy's group. Laura would have been a better teacher than me in some ways but worked great behind the scenes to strengthen our women and helped organize the ministry. Micah and Laura challenged and pushed me to be a better campus minister. I confess it felt hard to have weaknesses that matched someone else's strengths. Instead of seeing it as God intends, where we complement one another, it can feel like a competition. Sometimes leaders can get caught in a trap of thinking they have nothing to learn from someone younger. God, forgive us. Even though it wasn't easy, I know I tried to learn from them and take their input. I'm sure I failed at times, but I know I recognized their strengths and gifts and wanted to learn. My experience of not being specifically trained to be a campus minister had a dark and light side. The dark side was it produced insecurity. The light side was it made me open to learning from others. It took prayer and quiet time with God to make sure the light side won out.

Laura pursued professional work in line with her master's degree. Micah decided to get back into campus ministry and took a job at Western Kentucky University (WKU). He was our first apprentice that we placed in a campus ministry position. I was ecstatic! It felt like five years of work since 2006 had paid off. Of course, Ole Miss and Rebels for Christ (RFC) had been blessed the whole time, but now we were able to be a blessing to another ministry and be part of a kingdom vision greater than ourselves like we had experienced going to Haiti. This is why Paul's words in 2 Corinthians 10:15-16 have stood out to me for years now. *"Our hope is that, as your faith continues to grow, our sphere of activity among you will greatly expand, so that we can preach the gospel in the regions beyond you."* Paul wanted the Corinthians' faith to continue to grow, which represented the Ole Miss campus and the RFC ministry to me. But he also knew that the growth of their faith would cause kingdom growth beyond Corinth and thus, beyond Oxford. Micah at WKU was proof to me that these verses were living and active.

In the spring semester of 2011, we were surprised by a couple that moved to Oxford, Drew and Kelcy Messick. Drew had a full-time job, but Kelcy agreed to work with us as a female apprentice. Kelcy was the first to really help us get a freshmen small group going. I still wince recalling her request to meet with me and Eric because I was slow to act on her desire to implement the small group we both wanted. Regardless, I was thankful once the ball was rolling because we needed that pathway to connect better with our freshmen and help them connect better with each other.

In June 2013, we welcomed a new male apprentice, Deonte Watkins, to Oxford. I was excited to have Deonte because he had gone to Georgia Southern for undergrad and wanted to go to Harding School of Theology (HST) in Memphis to work on a ministry degree. It had a similar ring to my experience and Deonte had been blessed by a small group of disciples at his public university. Deonte was perhaps my first apprentice that was what I have termed more "traditionally conservative" than me. I believe we were both biblical conservatives in that we highly valued and respected the Bible as God's word and were in complete agreement on the core doctrines of the faith concerning Jesus as the Son of God, his death, burial, and resurrection, etc., but I know we saw the role of women differently in some areas and we even discussed our differing views on clapping in a worship service. Some of you will know exactly what I'm talking about when I mention a disagreement on clapping and some of you are probably laughing wondering how on earth we would even need a conversation on that subject.[49] *It all depends on your context.* The fact is, we had Christian students in our church tradition coming to Ole Miss who were taught that clapping was wrong.[50] Perhaps the verse about worshiping God in reverence and in awe from Hebrews 12:28 would have been used. Ironically, in Hebrews 12:22 we also see thousands and thousands of angels in joyful assembly. My point was not to make everyone clap, but that those so moved by the Spirit had the freedom to clap and those who didn't want to clap, certainly didn't have to. Now I'm not here to talk about how Deonte and I have continued to grow in our faith and

---

[49] I laugh at the silliness of the Sadducee's riddle for Jesus about the seven brothers who all married the same woman. See Mark 12:18-27. Paul warns about "endless genealogies" in 1 Timothy 1:4. Everyone has their issues!

[50] Don McGlaughlin, *Love First*, Abilene: Leafwood Publishers, 2017, 63-64. (Just in case you think I'm crazy.)

understanding on a variety of issues. I just wanted you to know about a practical issue that we faced. If you train an apprentice or are being trained as an apprentice, I'm sure you will discover your issues for discussion. *The main thing was that sometimes we had to agree to disagree, and we learned to love one another despite our differences.*[51] Our elders often got involved to guide us through what we could practically do. I credit the church's support of campus ministry as a primary reason why this issue had to be addressed. Whatever we did, I challenged us to do it for the glory of God. After finishing his time with us, I was so grateful to learn that Deonte had taken the campus minister position at Virginia Tech. Now it felt like we had some momentum.

Even still, I sensed that I was going to have to be more proactive in my pursuit of apprentices as there were not a lot of students coming to HST looking to be a campus minister, so I started visiting Harding University in Searcy, Arkansas. In March 2014, I visited Dr. Scot Crenshaw's class on Evangelism. By the end of the spring semester, we had hired Claire Allensworth to be our next female apprentice. She announced this on her social media: *"I cannot express how blessed I feel right now. I have officially been accepted as the new Rebels for Christ female apprentice at Ole Miss! I am so excited to work with the church in Oxford and students this coming fall. How incredible is the love of God!"*

I loved Claire's answer to one of our interview questions about her long-term ministry plans: *"God has called me to be a part of a full-time ministry where I can work to strengthen his people. The specific area where this will take place has been a mystery for me during my time at Harding. I never considered campus ministry as a possibility because of the lack of focus or emphasis on a Christian campus, but I can clearly see where my time at Harding has given me a love for this age of transformation. God is calling me to serve in a way that he served me during my college experience."*

Claire's experience was similar to mine at ACU. Campus ministry had not been on her radar at a Christian school and still might not have been if I had not come to her class that day. That's an amazing and scary thought. I remember Claire exclaiming after the 2015 conference in Austin, *"Where has this been all my life?!"* Claire also had a desire to serve in non-traditional roles for women (at least within some churches). I am thankful that Claire helped our ministry and church family wrestle with this challenging issue. Even after she left, our church leadership was still trying to articulate what we believed

---

[51] Deonte affirmed this when I consulted with him: "But the lesson that you taught me is one that I use even to this day—loving people that I have biblical or doctrinal disagreements with. If I had not learned that from you, I don't think I would have had a long career in ministry."

and what we believed the church and campus ministry could handle. As with the clapping issue, you could pull out one of Paul's verses about women (or wives) being silent in 1 Corinthians 14. But you could just as easily see women praying and prophesying in 1 Corinthians 11. Students and members tended to gravitate to one or the other because of their preferences. My point was to help both sides see that both were in Scripture and to learn to live with the tension—which is terribly hard to do in churches. We want black and white when Scripture is sometimes gray. I said I was thankful for Claire's help, and I truly meant it, but I know, at times, it came at a cost to her mental and emotional well-being. It was hard on her not knowing what she could and could not do. She did some things that were ok at the time, only to be told later by our elders that she could not do those things anymore. She came to me frustrated and bewildered numerous times. Claire, I want to honor you here and thank you for laying down your life to help our ministry and church wrestle with such an important issue as how to treat our young women who are looking for places to serve in our churches. We must keep pursuing this difficult issue in love for the sake of our daughters and granddaughters and female students.

During Claire's first year, I had begun raising support for my ministry and for the apprenticeship. By **April 1, 2015**, I was on a spiritual high having reached my goal. Here's what I wrote in my journal: *"Now I currently have no male apprentice on the horizon. I'm a little down, but after the way God has worked in other ways, I am confident he will raise up someone new. He is awesome and I am learning to walk by faith more, trusting him knowing he is at work even when I can't see it yet."* That month, I visited Dr. Crenshaw's class again and a student named Dalton Stamps reached out to me. We had found our next male apprentice. I loved Dalton's answer to the same question Claire answered above: *"My degree is in Bible and Family ministry. Basically, youth ministry. However, when I did my youth ministry internships, I felt much more drawn to the older teens. This time, around 15-18, when they are being given more and more of the reins on their lives, is a time when they are asking questions like 'Why does any of this God-stuff matter?' Campus ministry gets to defend the message at a time when students are building who they will be. I think that I can help in that mission."*

I would say that our ministry peaked during Dalton and Claire's apprenticeships. Dalton could help me focus on the guys and was great with the younger students. Claire was a great mentor and friend to our young women but was also creative and artistic and we found avenues for her to share those gifts with students. They both helped with our freshmen small groups and helped me plan events and get students to participate. Our numbers were higher and more consistent because of their presence. I was part of a team, training future campus ministers while we worked together to reach students at Ole Miss.

Dalton eventually became the campus minister at East Carolina University in 2018. Claire took an associate campus minister position at Arizona State University. When they moved on in 2017, my heart was full. The ministry was fulfilling my hopes and dreams not only for Ole Miss but for the larger kingdom work as well. To paraphrase what Paul said about Titus, God had put it into the hearts of these apprentices the same concern I had for the campus. I was excited to see who God would bring our way next, but similar to Tracey's health issue in 2006, there were storm clouds on the horizon.

Reflect

- *If you're in campus ministry, what steps can you take to make training apprentices a reality?*

- *If you're not in campus ministry, can you envision apprentices/interns still being a viable pathway for making disciples?*

41

My Toughest Student

August 2012: *"Feel like God is calling me to learn a hard lesson—that he can even work despite me. I love it when God works through me. It's harder to trust that he is still at work when I get in the way or don't perform up to mine or someone else's expectations. Eric told me yesterday to say with John the Baptist, 'I am not the Messiah.' I didn't want to hear that yesterday. I'm trying to hear it and accept it today."*

The odds were seemingly stacked against us from the beginning. When Paul started coming to RFC in the fall of 2012, Tracey and I were in the trenches with the twins. There is no doubt the ministry suffered at least a little during this time. There was certainly no extra time and energy for new ideas and initiatives with only a few hours of broken sleep every night. Kelcy, my female apprentice, was a big help, but we did not have a male apprentice at this time. I learned early on that Paul was creative and had lots of ideas. He would often stop by my office during the day to talk. Paul certainly taught me to be interruptible, which I have mentioned did not come naturally to me. We would talk about a lot of things but at some point, he would usually share an idea or two he had. Often it centered around an event that he thought we should offer to new students. I appreciated his heart because I wanted the same thing—new students. Only looking back can I see better where we diverged. It was all about the process. Paul was, in general, event-focused—something I did not consider myself very good at. I had *learned* to plan Welcome Week, our 2010 Conference, CRF nights, Haiti trips, and more but it wasn't a natural gift. I'll admit I was weary of event planning and didn't want to add another one to the list. I was focused on smaller things—meeting one new student for coffee and conversation. We both wanted new students, we just wanted to go about it in different ways.

Here are some things I journaled after a meeting with him. He had been in the ministry for a year.

June 7, 2013: *"Some things for me to work on:*

1. *Big vocabulary—avoid when possible (My theological training was showing though I had learned to pair it down over the years.)*
2. *Continue looking for connections in Greek system (which happened in the Fall of 2013)*
3. *Meet Paul weekly (I don't think this happened, but we often had short visits)*
4. *Make sure students don't walk into my office with ideas and leave defeated*
5. *Convey passion (I wanted him to see that I was passionate about my ministry even though in general, I did not often display that passion to the degree that he and others may have wanted.)*

For Paul to work on:

1. *More participation—small groups and retreats (I perceived, right or wrong, that Paul needed to be more invested in our existing ministry to give him more credibility with me and current student leadership. Then we could receive his new ideas better.)*
2. *Patience--Remember change often happens slowly*
   God, bless our friendship. Help things to get better as we trust each other more. Work for good!"

When I mentioned the idea of conveying "passion," it always struck me that when Jesus was asleep in the storm on a cushion in Mark 4, the disciples' response to him was, "Don't you care if we drown?" In other words, they are taking Jesus' ability to be at peace in a storm and misinterpreting it as a lack of care for them. Now I've already mentioned my inability to be at peace on a plane, so I still have much to learn from Jesus about this. *But it did resonate with me that sometimes we can misinterpret calm as not caring.* I wanted to work harder at revealing my internal passion so that Paul could see we were more alike than he thought. I'm not sure how successful I was.

A few days later I had lunch with Paul's dad. He told me something that should have made me seek immediate counseling with Paul—he was a doer and a feeler. I was a thinker and a reflector—meaning I liked to reflect on the things I was thinking about. We were exact opposites. Unfortunately, I continued with the way things were. I often wrestled with how much Paul seemed to care about the ministry, but he didn't seem to appreciate my approach. I know he had had a great experience in the youth ministry with our youth minister, Chad. Perhaps deep down he wanted the same kind of relationship with me. Perhaps he wanted campus ministry to be more like his youth ministry experience. I wish I had taken the time to discuss this with him more. I wish I had talked with Chad more about this too.

At some point in 2015 or 2016, my apprentices Dalton and Claire, with Eric, Jim, and myself, gathered in Eric's office for a meeting that I believe Paul had called. Jim was a new elder who had joined the campus ministry team. On this particular day, Paul's patience with me gave out, and every frustration that he had with me boiled over. He said things I'm sure he later regretted. Thankfully, I don't remember much about the meeting except the intense emotion. It was traumatic for me as I wrestled with whatever part I absorbed and did remember at the time. I was also thankful that Jim stepped up to take the brunt of Paul's frustrations after that day. I know Jim said something to me that helped me feel like he had my back and that I couldn't be dealing with regular conflicts with Paul. We still had conversations from time to time, but it was awkward and strained for a while.

As if often the case, death has a way of changing our perspective on many things, including difficult relationships. After an especially difficult funeral in June of 2018, I spoke with Paul briefly afterwards and later texted this: *"Hey I don't know if what I said after the funeral came out right. Tough days like this make me reflect on a lot of things. But I do appreciate you caring about the campus ministry and wanting what's best. Even if we see it differently sometimes, I am thankful you are my brother in Christ, both of us working towards the same goal. Love you, brother."* I don't remember what I said, but he quickly replied: *"Oh you're good, I promise. I knew what you meant and yes, I'm thankful for you too and love you also."*

It felt like we had forgiven each other and found some peace with our differences. I thanked God for this grace. Every minister will have their toughest teen, college student, or church member at some point. I hope you can learn from some of my mistakes, be more proactive and lean into these people, investing more time in them *when appropriate*. In campus ministry, summer tends to be a good time to do this before our energy needs to shift back to a new school year and new students.

Reflect

- *Who has been your toughest student or church member? Watch and pray for an opportunity to make things better.*

42

Faith Becoming Sight

"For we live by faith, not by sight." 2 Corinthians 5:7

"By God's grace, a team from WOLFLIFE (Arkansas State) will start a new campus ministry at the University of Washington in Seattle next summer. That team was prayed for by Milton Jones who led a team that planted a campus ministry at UW close to 40 years ago." 2016 Campus for Christ Conference

At the same 2016 conference, another group of ministries invited me to their fall retreat to share some lessons on evangelism of all things. I felt more equipped than ever, but "Casey" and "evangelism" were not two words that naturally went together. As things were starting up in Seattle on the West Coast, it was neat to see ministries near the East Coast getting together as well. Here is what I wrote for my supporters after the retreat:

"So much of life is walking by faith. You have to step out in faith and take risks like Peter getting out of the boat. You have to trust someone enough to do something that may appear crazy and often is. But God rewards our faith and we get to see him do some amazing things. We step out in faith, but then we see what God is doing.

"This happened to me in a very real way in November. But first, we have to go back a ways...a long way back to 2004. It was my first year of campus ministry and I attended my first campus ministry conference in Morgantown, West Virginia. Jason Locke was the campus minister there, a friend of mine thanks to his deep friendship with my campus minister, Scott Karnes. At the end of a great weekend, I remember that we prayed for all the campuses in the Northeast that did not have a campus

ministry from our brotherhood and there were many. I remember through the challenge given and our prayers that I committed to being part of the solution in some way.

"Then in 2007, Rebels for Christ took a spring break trip back to West Virginia and we also prayer-walked the Maryland campus on a day trip to D.C. Maryland was one of those campuses that did not have a campus ministry (they were kicked off in the 80s because of abuses associated with the Boston movement). And this time last year, you may recall that Dalton Stamps, Eric Dahl, and I visited the Maryland campus and the University Park Church of Christ where their campus minister, Kevin Rivera, now works! What an amazing answer to prayer after 30 years without a campus minister!!

"Then this past summer at our ministry conference, God brought 4 campus ministers together in a special way: Kevin at Maryland, Rusty Jordan at Delaware, Harrison Gibbs at East Carolina, and Deonte Watkins at Virginia Tech. Some of you will remember that Deonte was an apprentice here with me for two years. God has answered our prayers because he is now leading his ministry and how intriguing is it that Virginia Tech, Maryland, Delaware, and East Carolina are a gateway to the Northeast? These 4 ministers committed to doing a retreat this fall and bringing their students together for a special weekend of fellowship, teaching, and renewal--which brings me back to November.

"I was super blessed to be invited to facilitate the weekend for these 4 beautifully diverse ministries. I watched Kevin and Deonte and everyone else loving and serving one another all around me. I realized that God was giving me a chance to see the result of my faith and prayers. My faith was becoming sight. I was able to catch a glimpse of what God had been doing all those years when I couldn't see what he was doing-- that the prayers offered with a mustard seed of faith in 2004 and 2007 were bearing fruit in 2016. And I say this almost every month, but YOU are part of this amazing ministry with your prayers and financial support. You allow me to train students to be disciples of Jesus and you help me shape their hearts to care about other campuses that don't have what we are super blessed to have here at Ole Miss. I can't wait to see what God does next!"

I hope you notice the history I am leaning on in this experience. My first conference and the spring break trips played an important part in how I interpreted this retreat in which one of my apprentices was now the campus minister. I saw God at work in a special way. Events that could have seemed random were not random to me. That will become even more important later.

Reflect

- *What is an experience you've had where God allowed you to see how your past prayers and work produced fruit in the present?*

43

Every Tribe, Every Nation

"After this, I looked, and there before me was a great multitude that no one could count, from every nation, tribe, people, and language, standing before the throne and before the Lamb." Revelation 7:9

August 2010: *"Milton told the story of a campus minister who baptized a black man in the 70's. Elders told him black people didn't have souls. He baptized another black man and elders threatened his job."*

We love the earlier verses in Ephesians 2 related to our salvation.[52] But we must remember what the point of our salvation is—by one faith, one Lord, and one baptism, we are placed in a community with everyone from every tribe and nation who is different from us but also follows Jesus. Remember the Rwandan genocide and the American Civil War? Our tribe was more important than Jesus. Rich and poor, Jew and Gentile, male and female, and—of course, for a ministry in the deep South— black and white can all worship together under the Lordship of Jesus. Paul anticipates the conflicts that are bound to arise between different groups:

"For he himself is our peace, who has made the two groups one and has destroyed the barrier, the dividing wall of hostility...His purpose was to create in himself one new humanity out of the two, thus making peace, and in one body to reconcile both of them to God through the cross, by which he put to death their hostility." Eph 2:14-16

---

[52] "For it is by grace you have been saved, through faith...not by works, so that no one can boast. For we are God's handiwork, created in Christ Jesus to do good works...." Ephesians 2:8-10

Every Tribe

In other words, it is not diversity for diversity's sake. It is diversity for Jesus' sake. With this in mind, our ministry was mostly white for several years. I would even say I didn't think much about race in those early years negatively or positively. I want to make sure you understand this is not a noble statement but rather an indictment. There were many reasons for this:

1. Fear of how to tackle a sensitive issue given my desire to avoid conflict
2. Lack of vision and prayer for the new humanity Paul sought in all his church plants
3. Incompetence having never been directly coached on how to pursue a healthy community of black and white students
4. My preference to stay ignorant given all the other issues I was facing with Tracey's health and the "regular" struggles that come with doing ministry.

Over the years, I've heard several comments related to church growth that encourage homogenous groups because they grow faster. This deserves a larger conversation, but I just want you to consider that in my experience, being open to Spirit-led diversity may or may not numerically grow your ministry.[53] Nevertheless, the community will more accurately reflect the "every tribe, every nation" vision that God has for his people, and it is beautiful to behold no matter the numbers.

Our campus ministry had no idea the ripple effects that would occur when God sent us an interracial family in 2010. I often told the story of the Lyons' family to our students. Here's how it happened. One of our student leaders, Nick invited a female student nicknamed Soup.[54] Soup had a friend named Sam Lyons who started coming with her to Bible studies. As we cared for Sam, his family got connected to our church family as well—Horace and Julie with Sam's siblings Joey and Jessica. Joey came around some, but Jessica

---

[53] "Usually when things grow fast and large, they also grow homogeneously...we like to be around people who look and think like us. Our big visions for multiculturalism and reconciliation will make their way into the church only when they are first lived out in real relationships, out of our homes and around dinner tables and in our living rooms. Perhaps this is why Jesus begins it all by sitting around a table with a Roman tax collector, a Zealot revolutionary, a fisherman, a Pharisee, and a prostitute." Shane Claiborne, *The Irresistible Revolution: 10th Anniversary Edition,* Grand Rapids: Zondervan, 2016, 314.

[54] I mentioned her previously in the "*Church Politics 202*" chapter.

was very much a part of the youth ministry. It was a unique situation as Horace and Julie were both blind and Horace was confined to a wheelchair and dealt with a lot of health issues. He was still very accomplished as a teacher and professor. Over the years, we prayed for this family many times, cared for them when they moved houses, and even took up a special contribution for them from our church family when times were really tough. As Sam graduated, Jessica joined the campus ministry and was very much a servant leader. She worked at our coffee house as a barista, was a leader on our trips to Haiti, and served very well as an intern. Because we had loved Sam and Jessica well, Jessica felt safe with us even though we were still a mostly white ministry. By the time Jessica graduated, I would guess ten of her friends had come through RFC with us. I'm sure we could have done more to help Jessica and her friends feel like they truly belonged in RFC, but loving her family well had allowed the Spirit to bless us with more diversity and work out the implications of new creation and new humanity among us.

The other big thing God did was send Deonte to be our apprentice in 2013. I remember Deonte helping us at our recruitment table for freshman orientation and black students would actually stop and talk to us about our ministry. As welcoming as I thought I was to every student who came by, it still seemed important to students that they were represented by someone like them. Just as I tried to have female students help me reach incoming female students, having black representation helped us reach black students and made our ministry legitimate in their eyes. Again, I couldn't create this or force this, but I believe God saw that we were a safe place for people who looked different from me and honored us with these beautiful people. God also used Deonte to baptize Joey Lyons into Jesus.

Even as I was facing some difficult issues in my ministry in 2017, Lendy connected me with Sherod Bryant, preaching minister for the Rivers Hill church in town. I was super blessed to have the opportunity to preach for them on a Sunday in July. Here is what I wrote in my journal: "*Very humbled that they collected $128 for a love offering and gave me $250 for speaking. Had lunch with Sherod. Maggie said she made a friend today with a little girl named Paris. The most important thing today was allowing our kids to experience that with us thanks to Tracey—to know that we love people whose skin color is different and that we love and accept one another. Thanks for building the bridge Lord through Sherod!*"

By October, I was able to get Sherod to come to share a message at the Student Center on my 40th birthday. Even though Deonte and Jessica had moved on, their legacy was still evident in our ministry. Sherod also started coming with us to Haiti and bringing others. In February 2018, I had a text conversation with Marlon, a young black man and brother in Christ who had been part of the ministry in my early days in Oxford. Our conversation summed up the beauty of what God was working on among us:

Casey: Me and Sherod keep talking. Someday God is gonna bring black and white together and it will be a beautiful thing.

Marlon: That was powerful brother and I thank you for that. I talk to Durward (elder) as much as I talk to you. And I just shed a tear or two. But it wasn't tears of sadness it was tears of joy, hope for a better tomorrow. And for the love and the compassion that you and he have shown me and have not given up on me. And just like MLK, we shall overcome and his dream is not dead.

Casey: Amen! God is gonna bring us together at the end so we better start practicing now.

I believe this last statement was something I had gotten from Sherod, Lendy or both. God was knitting our tribes together over eight years of deepening investment into new humanity—and it had all started with one student's invitation.

Every Nation

But what about the nations?

Thanks to some contacts on campus, our ministry started connecting with more international students in 2016. The university saw how important it was for international students to get connected and feel like part of the campus community. If they had a good experience, they would go home and tell their friends and more of them would come to Ole Miss. Christians were the best at signing up for this good work. Rusty at Delaware actually connected me with a man named Greg Swinney who did a lot of work with international students. Greg worked with a group called The Rise Project to give out grants to ministries wanting to reach international students with the gospel. I applied and we were blessed to receive a grant. Two students, Keri and Reed, were a big help working with these students and had a big heart for them. I explained this in my grant proposal:

"Last summer a door was opened on campus. I was at the large kickoff event in August and was able to shuttle and meet many international students. My family was able to be a host family for someone from India who is Hindu and someone from Gambia who is Muslim. I also had connections with a Kenyan and her friend from

Brazil. The Indian student wanted to go on our mission trip to Haiti this summer but was concerned about the travel ban and did not think it wise. We have another young lady here from Tanzania teaching Swahili and lives at our Student Center where we house mostly believers in Jesus. So I believe we have done a pretty good job engaging these students. We know where to find them now and they know we love Jesus and are willing to participate in spiritual events with us. Now we hope to engage these students and others we will reach in the fall in a deeper spiritual way and invite them to consider Bible studies and Friend Speak conversations. An intern would be a huge help to organize this and engage both our campus ministry and church family in relationships with international students."

With Keri and Reed's leadership, we took international students to football games, had them in our homes, drove them if they needed a ride, let them cook us food, and even got to start reading the Bible with a few of them. Because international students were seekers and had no connection to Christian tradition, they didn't tend to show up at any of our regular events that were predominantly American. This didn't bother me as I knew the dynamics involved that made this hard to overcome in a short amount of time. However, as important as this work felt to me, they didn't get counted in our regular Bible studies on Sunday morning or Wednesday night. This will become important in a few more chapters. Greg was a great encourager as I found my passion for students coming to Ole Miss from every nation. Tyler Ellis told me that in Tom Phillips' book, *The World at Your Door*, he identified international ministry on the college campus as "The Reverse Great Commission" because, at universities around the country, the world was coming to us through international students. If we began sharing our love and faith with them, it was more and more likely they would someday become followers of Jesus. And whether they stayed in America or went back to their home country, the gospel would spread the way Jesus intended. The vision for every tribe and every nation was compelling and I was thankful our ministry was part of it at Ole Miss.

Reflect

- *Evaluate the diversity of your relationships and your ministry. Would you rather grow a larger homogeneous group or a smaller heterogeneous group? Sift through your motives for each.*

- **Respond**: *Get on campus (or in your community) and find the international office and look for connections with international students and partner with other organizations that look different from your ministry.*

44

The Day I Almost Got Fired

"Conflicts on the outside, fears within." 2 Corinthians 7:5

January 2012: *"I know God wants me to keep speaking up in those moments where I would prefer to shrink back. I must trust that I will discover God is there with me, helping me. Sometimes I will cause trouble and sometimes I will be a salty blessing."*

February 2012—*Text from Lendy after he spoke at a funeral: "Thanks for prayers. I love you, brother. There is no one on this planet I'd rather be doing ministry with."*

March 2013—*Lendy wrote yesterday: "I just wanted you to know I love you. It would be fine with me if we could do ministry together until we croak!"*

It was now February 2017. I couldn't believe that Lendy and his family were moving. As my journal indicated, we had this optimistic, almost naïve belief that we would do ministry together forever. God had blessed our David and Jonathan friendship so much since 2006. I'll let him tell that story of why they moved but suffice it to say they needed a change. I had the privilege of preaching for one of his final Sundays with our church. The message I shared was actually an old sermon I had preached back in 2012. I do not recall any particular feedback on it then good or bad (cue ominous music). I refined the sermon a little bit but there were no major changes. It was entitled "Extremists for Love" based on Matthew 5:43-48 and a quote from Dr. Martin Luther King: *"These are extreme times. The question is not whether we will be extremists, but what kind of extremists we will be. Will we be extremists for hate or for love?'*[55] I saw it as a tribute to Lendy and his vision for racial reconciliation.

There are two parts of my message that I want to share here. The first was a story I got from Shane Claiborne, the man I had heard in person at our 2011 conference, and his book, *Irresistible Revolution.*

"There was an Iraqi woman whose son and husband were killed by a police officer…an American police officer. They eventually caught the police officer and brought him before the court. In court, as the judge considered the sentence of the police officer, the woman spoke: 'He took my family away from me, and I still have a lot of love to give, and he needs to know what love and grace feel like— so I think he should have to come to visit my home in the slums, twice a month, and spend time with me so that I can be a mother to him, so that I can embrace him, and he can know that my forgiveness is real.'"[56]

Can you imagine doing this? Here it is important to note that this came from Shane's experience in Iraq with the local people. It speaks to the radical forgiveness that is only possible in Jesus, instead of resentment, revenge, and bitterness. This woman was an extremist for love.

Here is the second part which includes the landmine I both created and stepped on. "You notice what Jesus says in verses 46-47: *'If you love those who love you, what reward will you get? Are not even the tax collectors doing that? If you greet only your brothers, what are you doing more than others? Do not even pagans do that?'* Remember Jesus getting in trouble for hanging out with tax collectors and sinners? Jesus gives them and us a very chilling reminder—you are just like the people you hate, if you cannot get outside of your group. The Father's love keeps the church from being just another social club or cult. The Father's love gently pushes us into uncomfortable situations where we must look into the eyes of those who do not share our skin color, our political agenda, or our understanding of the Bible. Hate allows us to keep people at arm's length. Love causes us to get too close for comfort. Thanks in large part to the national media's daily lessons in fear and hate, we depersonalize, dehumanize, and demonize the Father's children around the world who may indeed be our enemies, but who nonetheless need to know that they have a Father and a

---

[55] Martin Luther King Jr., *Letter from Birmingham Jail*, USA: *Penguin* Books, 2018, 19.
[56] Shane Claiborne, *The Irresistible Revolution (10th Anniversary Edition)*, Grand Rapids: Zondervan, 2016, 264.

family that loves them. This is extreme. Shane Claiborne told a story that forced me to personalize Iraq and war. 'I remember visiting one of the hospitals in Iraq. The doctors walked us by bed after bed of children who had been injured or killed in the bombings. I saw a little girl shaking in her bed, asking over and over, "What did I do to America? What did I do to America?"' Shane didn't stay in his group. You see, I can't hate Iraq and love war any longer when I hear stories like this, can you?"[57]

There were two interesting things about the context of this sermon. First, national politics had changed since I had preached in 2012. It's only a hunch but I tend to believe that played a part in how my sermon was received. Second, I got the most positive comments I think I have ever gotten after a sermon. I got encouragement in person, by email, by phone call. A dear sister Norma shared this: *"Wanted to say that I really enjoyed your message on Sunday. It was almost like Lendy was standing there...I do hope we will continue to hear the Word as it relates to reconciliation and the like. Thanks and keep allowing God to grow you."* I was so thankful that I could encourage Norma. She was one of the few black members in our congregation. But the lack of any negative comments was troubling. Something didn't feel right.

I got a message from Eric a couple of days later letting me know someone with negative comments was coming to see me. We met in the prayer room of the Student Center. I was very tense and anxious. I do not recall much about our discussion, but I do recall this person saying: "If it was up to me, I would fire you." I was taken aback by that. I knew that wouldn't happen, but it was still scary to hear. This man was visibly upset, and I learned a little about why. I wish I could say that there had been more of a dialogue— that he had asked me questions about why I used those examples. I wish I had talked more about listening to Shane at the 2011 conference—that he wasn't a fanatic for anyone other than Jesus, in my view. I wish I had asked more about his experiences. I should have asked before that day. I wish I had asked him to read *Mere Discipleship* or *The Irresistible Revolution* with me though that would have been scary too. If I had been wiser, maybe I would not have used those quotes as a way to honor him. I think the fact that I had preached the same general sermon without negative consequences prevented me from considering that we were not the same church we had been five years earlier. And that's my incompetence for not recognizing all of this. I do know that

---

[57] Shane Claiborne, *The Irresistible Revolution (10th Anniversary Edition)*, Grand Rapids: Zondervan, 2016, 265.

all I really wanted to do was honor my brother Lendy for the 11 years we had worked together and preach a message that was biblical and indicative of his ministry.

To this man's credit, the issue was never brought up again and I appreciated him for moving on. But it felt like we swept the issue under the rug, so things still felt strained and awkward. Also, my collection of illustrations and stories no longer felt safe to use, and going forward I was fearful to use anything that felt slightly controversial. At some point it hit me I wasn't in trouble for anything related to campus ministry—I was in trouble for what I had preached. In general, preaching is usually pastoral (gentle, inviting, patient) or prophetic (bold, challenging, urgent) and I often tended towards the pastoral. For years I wasn't sure how much the church listened to my monthly sermons, but they were sure listening that day. Ten plus positive comments but one really negative comment. It showed me the power of a prophetic word and the danger of a controversial illustration. Honestly, it seems hard to be a prophet who preaches weekly in an established church. I wonder if that's part of the reason my sermons are usually pastoral. I have immense respect for any preacher who must get up week after week and speak the word of God in truth and love.

Reflect

- *When have you gotten in trouble for something you said, taught or preached? What was the controversy? Would you do anything different?*

45

The Hospital Haunts Us

"For our light and momentary troubles are achieving for us an eternal glory that far outweighs them all." 2 Corinthians 4:17

Tracey on Facebook*: "Hey friends/prayer warriors…I just wanted to ask for some prayers. Thought I was having stomach ulcer pains. Had a CAT scan where the doctor found a bowel obstruction. Because I've had so many surgeries over the past decade, the adhesions have most likely constricted a part of the bowel. Before surgery, the doctor wants to try an NG tube in hopes that it will relax the obstruction. Also, please pray for Casey as he is stepping up once again in a big way to take care of our sweet kiddos while my body fights against itself."*

This was in 2015. Just a few weeks after Tracey had taken a special trip to celebrate her 40th birthday, we were rudely reminded that her body, especially her abdomen, could have a mind of its own. Thankfully, the NG tube (that they force down your nose) worked, surgery was avoided, and she was able to come home. It was a victory for sure but a fragile one. It felt like if she took one wrong turn, her body would betray her again.

We did get a reprieve but in March 2017, I sent this to my elders because she was facing another issue:

"We got some bad news at the doctor. Most of you will remember about a year and a half ago, Tracey came to an elder meeting to share what life is like for her and us. Much of that hasn't changed and maybe even gotten harder in some ways.

"For example, this past November, Tracey had a procedure done to try and stop some irregular bleeding. We were hopeful that this would solve it, but an ultrasound

yesterday confirmed to her doctor that the procedure did not work. Now he is recommending a partial hysterectomy which will mean her being cut open yet again (though not as large of an incision). This will also mean a day or two in the hospital and of course recovery time at home. We are still hoping that her parents will be moving to Oxford in the near future. Pray for this and for their house to be sold asap! We keep praying for healing and are trying to trust that this is the path to some physical healing. Many if not all of you know what it's like to live with some kind of struggle that is not easily resolved and won't be fully resolved until Jesus returns.

"Thank you for the grace you have extended to me and Tracey as we have juggled parenting, health complications, and our ministry here as best we can. We know God is at work for good and that his grace is sufficient despite our weakness.

Love to you all,

Casey and Tracey"

It is hard to read those words "…won't be fully resolved until Jesus returns." At some point in life, most followers of Jesus realize that some things won't be fully made right until Jesus comes back. It was hard to admit that about Tracey's body.

Our elders and church family had really shown us tremendous grace over the years, but after 2006 and the IVF process, I was afraid that everyone's patience with us was growing a bit thin. I had no real evidence for this, thankfully. It was just a fear because the family and ministry tension were always there. But then our situation got worse. In April, the partial hysterectomy surgery performed by Dr. Hunt (who had brought Maggie and Moses into the world) had gone well and he had cleaned up her abdomen the best he could, but he had also moved a lot of bowel around. She had eaten mostly a liquid diet up until Easter and then she splurged thinking it was safe. Here is something I wrote later about what happened next:

"It's really hard to see someone you love suffer. This third trip to the hospital is where I really got to see Tracey's pain. She was having pain in her abdomen again and briefly fainted at home on the way to the bathroom as I walked with her. We decided we better go to the ER. When we arrived, she sat down in a seat where they took her blood pressure. I never heard the number but thought someone later said 70/40. I had never seen them rush someone from the lobby to a room that fast. But when your BP is low, it's hard to get an IV started and they wanted to start TWO because she needed a lot of fluids. They stuck her way too many times until they finally got the lines in. It looked and sounded like torture as she cried out in pain. She had a test

done and they determined she needed the NG tube again that goes down your nose to your stomach. She had just had this and was scared at the thought of having to go through that again. But she fought back knowing this would help her avoid surgery. By this time, I could not sit there and watch them hurt my wife again, so I walked out feeling faint and let Eric stay with her. When I came back in, the tube was in place and a big tear was coming down her face.

"Once she was stable, I headed off to see her parents who were taking care of our kiddos and having supper at McDonald's. As I was leaving the hospital and driving to meet them, I noticed an amazing sight in the sky. To the east, there was a rainbow with a huge billowing orange and yellow cloud blocking most of the rainbow, but the legs were brilliant in color. To the west, the sun was beginning to set behind a wall of clouds as a silver lining formed around each cloud with beautiful yellow colors in the sky. I experienced a wide range of emotions in those few seconds. I knew what God was trying to say. I got choked up, I was in awe, I was frustrated because here was this beautiful display and I had just witnessed my wife suffering terribly. It was jarring because the two events didn't seem to go together. But I knew what God was saying: 'Casey, I'm still here. I haven't left you. I haven't left your wife.'"

If it had just been the hospital stay before we got married, if it had just been the appendix in 2006, if it had just been the IVF process, if it had just been these more recent hospital stays, Tracey's suffering would have been more acute with a clear starting and ending point. But the compounding effect of all of these trials often left us overwhelmed and wondering, "How long, O Lord? How much can one woman, one marriage, and one family endure?" If we had gotten our hopes up after the 2015 hospital stay, we were certainly less hopeful now. Is this what life was going to be like? Was Tracey going to have to go back to the hospital every few months or years to deal with this issue? The whole situation left us very unsettled. I tried to trust God and the rainbow, but it was so, so hard.

Reflect

- *What is an ongoing spiritual, mental, emotional or physical trial in your life?*

46

Defining Success

"We have renounced secret and shameful ways; we do not use deception, nor do we distort the word of God." 2 Corinthians 4:2

September 2006*: "Let go of numbers—numbers can drive you crazy in ministry. I've thought too much about having a big campus ministry. I need to focus on the one."*

As I went back through my journals, it was interesting how the idea of success came up every few years. I think it is something we all struggle with and want to know somewhere deep in our souls—did I do good work? Am I successful? Do others, whose opinion I value, see me as successful? Of course, this approach at best focuses on what we think (which can be flawed and biased), and at worst, it focuses on what others think who are, you guessed it, flawed and biased. Then there's the question—how do you even define success? Money, baptisms, followers on your social media platform, number of education degrees, number of students you have on average weekly? Could there be another way to define success? I believe so but we will need to wander through the wilderness of my ministry to get there.

It's here that I want to start by explaining that any success we have is often measured in terms of **addition or multiplication**. You will have to decide which you will measure because it will make all the difference. Steve Shadrach helps us imagine that if a great evangelist brought 1,000 people to Jesus every day, it would still take him tens of thousands of years to reach the entire world. That's addition ministry. That's event-focused ministry. It sounds great at the beginning, but it takes too long in the end. But, if I brought one person to Jesus and discipled him for a year and then in year two, we each brought another person to Jesus and made a disciple, the chain reaction of multiplication would begin and the world could be won to Christ in just thirty-three years.[58] Logic and Jesus' ministry should draw us towards multiplication, but the fact is, it is very hard to resist the temptation of addition.

In September 2007, I read *This Beautiful Mess* by Rick McKinley. I wrote this: *"Most convicting so far was Rick's words on levels versus dimensions. I am very much still a levels minister. I want to get to the next level personally, professionally, etc. I care way too much about numbers and numerical growth—the next level. What would it be like to not care about numbers but to be free to care for those who came?"* Levels teaches addition. Dimensions teaches multiplication.

It should be required reading for every minister to read Rick's chapter on levels versus dimensions entitled "A Dimension of Being." You can see back in 2007, I was fixated on the level of numerical growth. If we had 40 students, I wanted 50. If we had 60, I wanted 70. This taught me to never be happy with who came. This is addition, not multiplication. Now I am a big proponent of the phrase I got somewhere, "holy discontent." Without holiness, the discontent was just discontent. And that can leave you cynical, critical, and just plain unhappy. The numbers game also taught me to focus on *events*—successful events that would bring in more students. Those students would come back and bring their friends who would later bring their friends and we would have a huge ministry and I would be honored and respected by my students, my church, and my peers. This had the negative side effect of teaching me to believe that one-on-one or small-group Bible studies weren't as important. If I was going to let any plates stop spinning and drop to the ground (remember my growth review), it was going to be those smaller studies. God forgive me.

By February of 2009, my definition of success was starting to change for the better.

1. *Ministry contains people who wouldn't be together if it wasn't for Jesus.*
2. *Disciples are being made. Transformation is evident in at least one.*
3. *Students see the campus as mission field and themselves as missionaries.*
4. *Students are inviting other students.*
5. *Ministry is dependent on God in prayer (prayer room had started).*
6. *Focus is on faithfulness, not numerical growth.*

---

[58] Steve Shadrach and Paul Worcester, *The Fuel and the Flame*, Fayetteville: Center for Mission Mobilization, 2021, 29.

The engineer in me liked quantitative results. The number of students in a Wednesday night Bible study was much easier to determine than how many students had actually connected with Jesus and his word in those thirty minutes. This was the realm of qualitative data. If we really wanted quantitative data, better questions like these would have helped:

- How many students are reading their Bible or praying at least one day a week?
- Shared their faith this past week?
- Served a friend or stranger?
- Did something courageous for Jesus?
- Loved someone in a difficult relationship?
- The possibilities are endless!

This was before Milton's talk at the 2009 conference where he spoke about how much we invest in circles 4, 5, and 6 (levels/big events) but that discipleship only occurs in circles 1,2, and 3 (prayer, one-on-one, and small group studies). Still, in 2009, I didn't know how to articulate everything I was learning and how to cast a vision for strategic change. But I knew this: *If Jesus was regularly investing in twelve students while occasionally caring for strangers and the crowds, why wasn't I modeling my ministry off of his?*

In August 2011, I journaled about the first big gathering of the semester. This is an annual emotional roller coaster for campus ministers because of all the planning before the semester, the anticipation of new students, the execution of all the welcome week events, and then the follow up to keep the momentum going. I believe it was Tim Stafford who said, "Campus ministry is like planting a church every year," and I remember thinking, "That's why this feels so hard."

"There are so many struggles that come with being in my position.
1. *Expectations—I expect a lot of students to come tonight, but what if they don't?*
2. *Competition—We have to compete with other groups for students' attention (spiritual and otherwise).*
3. *Character and personality—For better or worse, a ministry is often evaluated based on the campus minister. I feel the pressure to be cool, to make students laugh, to wow them with my teaching.*

I've been praying that what would shine through is you, God. O Father, I want to crawl up in your arms. Please help me not to worry. Work in my weakness. I need you every hour. Apart from you, I can do nothing."

Can you hear the desperation? I felt this *every* fall semester. It was wearisome. And yet this was still focused primarily on events in Milton's 4, 5, and 6 circles, not discipleship.

April 2014: *"It has been 10 years since we moved from Abilene! Thank you, Father, for your faithfulness through it all. So many ups and downs and yet I'm still here serving and growing this ministry by your power. I know I am more courageous. I know you have made me a better dad and husband. I know I'm more evangelistic. I know I'm a better manager of a team. I know I have endured suffering and been refined by fire. You have worked in all things and brought so many good things into my life."*

Did you see my qualitative emphasis? I was more courageous, more evangelistic. How do you measure that? Only with the Spirit confirming it in my heart did I know it to be true. You can see that I also defined part of my success as being refined by fire and enduring suffering. Again, there's no metric for quantifying that, I just knew that I was growing.

In February 2016, at the height of our success as a ministry with two apprentices, a few interns, and a ministry of 70-80 students I wrote this: *"Lord, the desire to be successful is so easily felt. I feel it from the outside and I feel it from within my own heart. Please help me to die to success as the world defines it and teach me to simply be faithful to you. Then let the ministry chips fall where they will."*

It felt like I was learning not to get caught up in the numerical success we were having. I was grateful for everyone who came but no longer obsessed. I knew my job was to train my student leaders and a few students while reaching out to a few international students. That was my Twelve. Thanks to the Holy Spirit, I had learned to surrender much of my inner desire for worldly success. But the pressure from outside my own heart was just beginning to be felt. You will see the struggle for me and my leadership to define success in the chapters to follow. The problem was, I didn't know how to get my student leadership and the eldership out of the events/addition mindset. I needed a reset button and couldn't seem to find one.

The answer to defining success is found Matthew 3. I want to remind you that the Bible is not just history. We are told that the word of God is living and active. It's why I can speak about historical events in Matthew 3 today as if they are more than history. So, when the Father says, *"This is my son, whom I love; with him, I am well pleased."* do you think those amazing words could be meant for us also when we are baptized? Tod Vogt with *Mission Alive* shared this in a discipleship cohort so I want to credit him with this intriguing question. And I believe the answer is a resounding "yes!" Before Jesus preached the Sermon on the Mount, he was loved. Before he healed the paralytic, calmed the storm or did any other amazing thing, his Father was pleased with him. Before his ministry ever began, he was a son. Jesus already had his identity—so he didn't have to go out and prove himself to anyone. Are you with me? If you've been baptized, can you go back and remember when it was, where it was, and who baptized you? You know what I wish I had been told when I came up out of the water? "Casey, your heavenly father is saying—you are my son, I love you and I'm well pleased with you." Before I became a campus minister, I was a son. Before I ever taught a Bible class at the Student Center, I was loved completely. Whether I went to Haiti or not, my heavenly Father was already pleased with me. Do you see how this changes everything about how we define success? *The shocking conclusion of the gospel is that we are already successful, not because of what we do, but because of whose we are.* What if we lived out our successful identity in Jesus instead of going around trying to prove ourselves to everyone else? What if we did fewer events because there wasn't the pressure to have big numbers? What if we focused on multiplying a few students instead? What if we trusted God to make us competent? Yes, I still needed to grow and improve in some areas, but growth is healthier and more lasting when we remember our God-given identity. I wish I could go back and remind "2016 Casey" of his identity, before everything that happened next. I know God tried to remind me many times. It was just so hard to hear.

Reflect

- *How would you evaluate your success in life or ministry so far? Are the standards you are using helpful or harmful for the ministry?*

- **Resources:** *This Beautiful Mess by Rick McKinley. The Choice by R. Scott Rodin, Gary G. Hoag, & Wesley K. Willmer. You Are Special by Max Lucado is a wonderful children's book that is helpful within this context of success.*

- **Respond:** *Contact Mission Alive if you are interested in joining a discipleship cohort: tod@missionalive.org*

Section 4:

The Crucible

Crucible: a situation of severe trial, or in which different elements interact, leading to the creation of something new.

Let's begin this final, painful journey to something new.

47

The Beginning of the End

"Our conscience testifies that we have conducted ourselves in the world, and especially in our relations with you, with integrity and godly sincerity." 2 Corinthians 1:12

"Let us find some corner out of the wind and gather our strength—for the last lap." The Lord of the Rings[59]

Claire was our female apprentice for three years, 2014-2017, and Dalton was our male apprentice for two years 2015-2017 (his fiancé then wife, Danielle, was a big help as well). Their time in Oxford was coming to an end. Claire had found a wonderful ministry to join out at Arizona State. Here is the note she wrote our church family in April 2017:

"To my family in Oxford, I find myself experiencing a mixture of joy and sorrow as my time among you is coming to a close and a new path is spreading before me. I will be moving to Tempe to be a part of a team to start a new campus ministry at Arizona State University! This is an incredible opportunity to reach out to one of the largest campuses in the country and help revitalize our church family in Tempe. I hope you know that I take your wisdom, your guidance and your overwhelming love and your passion for campus ministry with me as I begin preparations for this new adventure. Pray that God will continue to claim every campus from Ole Miss to Arizona with his great power! With love, Claire"

Dalton and Danielle moved back to Huntsville, Alabama, at the end of the 2017 spring semester. I hoped they would find their way into campus

---

[59] J.R.R. Tolkien, *The Lord of the Rings*, New York: Houghton Mifflin Company, 1965.

ministry when the time was right. They did with Dalton becoming the campus minister at East Carolina University in 2018. Go Pirates!

As their futures were becoming clearer, mine was becoming clouded. Two huge things happened in June 2017 that would have a major impact on my ministry. First, Eric decided that he needed to go on a sabbatical as an elder so he could care for his mom, Elza. She had been a grandmother in the faith to me because she reminded me of my Grandma Coston. It seemed fitting since I was Eric's son in the faith. Then, soon after this, Jim told me that the elders were discussing the mission of Rebels for Christ (RFC) and that apprentices might be taken off the table as part of that mission. I cannot describe those words as anything other than a gut punch. I could not believe what I was hearing. It was so confusing. I didn't understand why that was being so seriously considered. I knew about the tension Claire's role created for us and there were plenty of other issues to work through, but the dam had finally broken. Somewhere along the way, the elders had begun to lose trust in me to lead the way I wanted. I tried to get some clarity, but I think Jim felt like he'd already said too much, and the conversation ended. I remember mowing my yard that afternoon and my mind would not stop the endless loop of why. I got a tightness in my chest that was a mixture of anxiety and anger. I do not blame Eric at all for leaving me at this time though I know he felt bad for leaving. It was like that time in 2006 when he had to leave me alone in the hospital waiting for Tracey to come out of surgery. He needed to be with his mom, honor her, and care for her as long as she was alive. I would have done the same. Our friendship never changed, but I had lost my contact elder and one of the primary shepherds of my soul and ministry for 13 years. Dale joined Jim as a new elder focused on campus ministry. They were good friends and I'm sure Jim began getting Dale up to speed on everything.

At this same time, Tracey's parents were finishing up their ministry in Austin, Texas, and looking to retire. We all agreed we would love to have them in Oxford with us. It would be a big help, and the kids would love it, but I was cautioned by some that I might want to discourage my in-laws from moving to Oxford and/or buying a house. I now know they could sense that the future was going to be difficult. I checked around for a few campus ministry positions but found nothing. I took it as a sign that God wanted me to stay put. Honestly, though, it was going to have to be the perfect position for me to consider somewhere else and I'm not sure I would have known what that looked like in 2017.

We officially invited Tracey's parents to move to Oxford so, the pressure was strong to stay put and do my best to make it work. I didn't feel like I could be the one to uproot my family from their home on Deerfield Drive, their church home, their school, and their friends. That is a tremendously difficult place to be in and so I did what I knew I could do—endure. But even under the surface of these legitimate personal reasons was a deeper struggle. I had naively thought, perhaps bordering on idolatry, that I would do campus ministry in Oxford forever. You mean even good things can be idols? Sadly, yes. I told myself I was doing it for Doug Sr., Kenny, Eric, or Lendy based on some hints of hope we had given each other over the years. I had never really considered that God might want to work another way. Looking back, I know this meant I wasn't going to be the one to end things. It was my one serious relationship in college all over again, but the magnitude was so much bigger. I was committed—to the bitter end.

P.S. **April 2018**: *"With her 3 sons at the bedside, mom (Elza) finished her course and got her rest. She passed in peace. Thanks for all your loving support across the months that have been so hard."* Eric

Reflect

- *Current Minister: When have you lost a key supporter of your ministry or when did your leadership decide that some things needed to change. How did it affect you?*

- *Future Minister: What have been some major changes in your life so far? How well did you handle the uncertainty regarding your future?*

48

Church Politics 301: Defender

"I have made a fool of myself, but you drove me to it. I ought to have been commended by you, for I am not in the least inferior to the 'super-apostles,' even though I am nothing." 2 Corinthians 12:11

"And we shouldn't be here at all, if we'd known more about it before we started. But I suppose it's often that way." The Lord of the Rings

In my first experience with church politics, I was just a participant. In my second experience, I was a mediator between students and elders. This time, I was the defender. I dug in and prepared for some important meetings with my elders. I was particularly focused on saving the apprenticeship if at all possible. I thought I had good reasons. I thought apprentices were better for me, better for the campus, and better for the kingdom! But maybe apprentices weren't better for the local church? It became clear that the elders and I had different ideas about some of our methods to reach the campus, but I was willing to go along with them to try and work things out. The elders certainly had more to think about than campus ministry. They were trying to figure out how campus ministry fit into the larger vision for the local church.

In early July, I compiled some thoughts for the elders that functioned as my opening arguments in defense of my ministry and the apprenticeship. I will say that when you are defending your ministry, you can come across as, you guessed it—defensive. When Paul defended his ministry, he said he sometimes thought he had made a fool of himself. It is hard to know where the line is between defending your ministry and getting defensive when things don't go the way you want. Defense is appropriate but getting defensive tends to hurt what you're trying to do. In what follows, I have tried to keep most of what occurred back in 2017 and let you wrestle with the tension.

First, I thought it wise to affirm the relationship we had built together. I thanked each elder individually for something specific and personal. For me it was important to emphasize our *relationship* with each other because ministry and mission were different from a bottom-line approach in business. Whatever decisions we made, I wanted it to be based on a broader perspective of what God was doing among us. Then I began my defense.

Firewall Dahl

"I received this document from Jim and Dale last week that is from the current eldership. I mentioned something about Eric's support of my ministry and Dale confirmed that Eric had defended some aspect of my ministry perhaps many times. I was unaware of this. Though I will always appreciate Eric's support of my ministry, the mission to Ole Miss is bigger than me or him. This mission is our mission. It is the primary mission of OCOC and all the elders."

It was not hard to believe Eric had defended my ministry many times. I was just unaware of much of it. I think Eric and I joked at some point about his name being "Firewall Dahl." I had made it as long as I had with minimal elder intervention because Eric had defended my ministry. I would soon learn the elders as a whole had been wanting to address these issues sooner but Eric, after all we had suffered through together, had placed a firewall around me so I could lead the ministry the best way I knew how. I was placed in a terribly difficult situation of trying to honor Eric for all he had done while at the same time showing that I was ready to defend my ministry apart from Eric.

Two Main Concerns

I expressed some agreement with their document and then I turned to my concerns:

"First, in the document you say, 'The coaching of apprentices and interns is more about the vision of having campus ministries all over the US rather than primarily reaching the Ole Miss campus.' I understand why you would make that statement based on your desire for me to teach more and be upfront. However the work of apprentices and interns is almost exclusively focused on students at Ole Miss. Most if

not all of our outstanding interns this coming year have been developed by Dalton or Claire in small groups and one-on-one mentoring. I want the work of apprentices and interns to be primarily about reaching the Ole Miss campus and connecting students to OCOC.

"The second concern I have is time. If I increase my teaching time, it could lead to less time with students in small group or one-on-one settings."

Notice here the struggle between levels 4, 5, and 6 versus 1, 2, and 3 as described by Milton.

I was trying to show how apprentices gave me time to do more of the things they wanted done, but I know they were concerned that my investment in apprentices (discipleship) distracted me from the mission to reach students (evangelism). It was a hard tension to resolve.[60]

Maintain One Apprentice

Then I went into the most important part of my defense:

"I believe we need to maintain one apprentice. Why? Because of Matthew 9:36-37— 'The harvest is plentiful but the workers are few.'

"a. Even with our primary focus on Ole Miss, we need more workers. Even if I am teaching more, we need more workers. Jesus' 'Come follow me' mission was focused on twelve. It will be hard for me to focus on more than 12 students outside of teaching. An apprentice will help us reach more students and disciple them here and now.

"b. Please keep in mind that Jesus called disciples because he would not be with them forever. Obviously, I will not be here forever. Who will reach the Ole Miss campus, the next generation when I am gone? In our brotherhood, we have trouble producing new campus ministers because our Christian schools do not produce campus ministers like they do other ministers (youth, preaching, etc).

"c. Because we have had tremendous success sending our apprentices. (I listed where our apprentices had ended up.) We are one of only three ministries I know of training apprentices. We have been a light to other campus ministries."

This last point focused on the larger kingdom work God was doing but I felt like it was still important to remind them that God was using us to bless

---

[60] I think we were also wrestling with whether we wanted addition or multiplication.

others. I felt like God had called me to be a creator and guardian of the mission.[61]

I had concluded the defense of my ministry. I ended with some really good reasons for keeping the apprenticeship. I felt like I had honored some of their requests while addressing my concerns. Though I had been hurt in June, God gave me the strength to share in a loving way by July. I was hopeful there could be some kind of compromise. I would take a greater leadership role, whatever that meant exactly, and the elders would allow me to continue training one apprentice.

A few days later, I received a detailed letter from the elders (which I have condensed):

"After listening to your input and discussing the 'Come Follow Me' mission proposal, we still believe the best direction for merging the RFC's focus and the OCOC's focus back to reaching the campuses of Ole Miss is to suspend the apprentice program. We want you to know we believe in you and know you can accomplish this redirected focus. We hear your concern that this will reduce the staff. We hope that this will give you more opportunities to interact more closely with the interns. (I believe there was a concern with the apprentices influencing interns more than me.)

"We will be working with you to reestablish an apprentice program in the future, as you take time to more clearly define delegated responsibilities for future apprentices. During some of your office time, you may begin developing a policy and instruction manual for an apprentice program. You will need to include a working agreement so the apprentice understands what's expected of him/her from day to day. We expect a lot of time in prayer and thought to be used to ensure this program is beyond reproach. Once this program has been developed you may bring it before the elders for vetting/approval. The elders' intention is to consider reinstating this program in May 2018, if it meets the needs of keeping the mission of OCOC and RFC the same."

Eric had been hands-off on the day-to-day details of my ministry though I tried my best to keep him in the loop with decisions I was making. We had been through so many fires together that we trusted one another and had great admiration for each other's lives of faith. But my elder leadership was

---

[61] "Mission is the expression of the church's deep, abiding beliefs. Mission provides the major standard against which all activities, services and decisions are evaluated. Mission is the preserver of congregational integrity. It is about God's love for the world, not about what I like or don't like about my church. A major function of the congregation's stewards is to be the creators and guardians of the mission." Peter Steinke, *A Door Set Open*, Herndon: The Alban Institute, 2010, 78.

different now. I now knew I had been given a lot of freedom as a campus minister over the years because of the firewall Eric had provided. Now, I was being scrutinized and put under a microscope. I felt like I was being micromanaged and no longer trusted to carry out my responsibilities though I had done nothing wrong morally, ethically, etc. Like I said earlier, somewhere along the way, the elders had lost some trust in me but also saw the mission differently.

I was hurt again. I really thought they would compromise. I shared and vented with trusted friends outside of Oxford. My fellow campus minister and Campus for Christ Board member, Chris Buxton, sent me this: "I'm very sorry and don't agree with the decision. But prayers for the Lord's shaping and transforming work in you as you pass through this season. Our most important seasons in life are almost never the happy ones. Blessings for peace and assurance."

It was even more bittersweet a week later when we said goodbye to my final apprentice in Oxford—Claire. Some of my parting words to her were these: *"Thank you for being God's answer to our hopes and dreams to reach students we may never know until eternity."*

Early in the fall, I got an encouraging email from Jim: *"Last night was great, good dinner, good service, and good singing. Again, it was great last night with 58 people in attendance. Great job."* I sincerely appreciated Jim's encouragement at the time, but I will say two things. First, it appeared to me that Jim was focused on events and to be fair, I was too in a way. I wanted the dinner and the worship time and my lesson to go well. But it felt like I was being evaluated as a minister based on those events. What if one or more of those things didn't go well? Did that reflect poorly on my leadership? Would that be a strike against reinstating the apprenticeship? Second, the fact that Jim mentioned how many were there is important. Intentional or not, I believe that taught me that part of my evaluation was based on how many students came. This was one area where our definitions of success seemed to diverge. I did not believe it was fair to make student attendance a primary or even secondary indicator of my ministry's success or failure. I had been through the ups and downs of student participation for thirteen years. I knew we always started with the most students and by late fall and spring, we would settle into our core group. So, if we started at 58 but ended up between 40-50 for the year (or even had a night of 30-something students, which occasionally happened with the perfect storm of tests, work, and Greek life), what did that say about me to my leadership? It had not meant much all the previous years, but it felt like it meant more now.

Reflect

- *How have you handled disappointment in your life and/or ministry so far?*

49

Under the Microscope

"If I must boast, I will boast of the things that show my weakness."
2 Corinthians 11:30

"You may know, or guess, what kind of tale it is, happy-ending or sad-ending, but the people in it don't know. And you don't want them to."
The Lord of the Rings

My working agreement was basically a contract between me and my elders. I hadn't paid much attention to it the previous thirteen years. It had come up when Tracey was in the hospital for a long time and there was some discussion about my vacation time when I went to Haiti. Maybe 2-3 times total in 13 years had I thought about it. But now I was under the microscope. Now I had to show that I could lead differently and make changes without apprentices. It was like my growth reviews of old on steroids. Here are some of the changes that stood out to me in the new working agreement summer 2017:

1. *"Every effort will be made to foster student involvement and loyalty to the Oxford Church of Christ so that they will be similarly committed to a congregation of the Lord's church when they leave Oxford."* I understood that our leadership wanted more students to be part of our church family. I wanted the same thing. This statement makes the most sense if your focus is only on students from our tribe, Churches of Christ. But our ministry had always been a strange mix of students from Churches of Christ,

multiple church traditions plus international students. For years, I had loved my church and invited students to be part of it, but at the end of the day, I let college students make the decision. For me, it was always a process. I wanted to meet students where they were, help them work through their issues over time, and do all I could to encourage them to be part of a church family—hopefully ours. This was the wisdom I had gained from my thirteen years. To me it was like parenting—you can make your children go with you to worship until they're eighteen, but after that, all you can do is pray, nudge, and invite. I thought I was doing almost everything I could to foster student involvement, but my leadership wanted more. I would encourage you to work with your leadership to discern your target mission audience, and the kinds of students you really want to reach, and to make sure you are on the same page. I should have had more discussions with them about that.

2. *"Creating a professional atmosphere."* We went through a season with students where we wanted our Wednesday night Bible class to feel like a Sunday morning worship service. Highly organized, planned, and structured. We wanted PowerPoint slides running before worship, we had a sound system and mics for our worship team, etc. As much as I liked those things and certainly believed in some degree of organization, I felt like we were spending too much time on things that didn't matter as much as relationships. Some students wanted this as well and I struggled to articulate my concerns with such an atmosphere. If I could go back, I would remind us of Jesus' words about the Sabbath and apply them to events: Events were made for students, not students for events. It felt to me like we were spending too much time on Milton's 4, 5, and 6 circles. We soon had an interim preacher named Carlus Gupton who would use phrases like, "Keep the main thing, the main thing" and that's what I wanted too. I knew that my gifts, limited time, and energy were focused on caring for students way more than creating a professional atmosphere. Again, I'm all for some organization and planning. I would just encourage you and your leadership to wrestle with this tension and have some open dialogue about what is best in your context and find a healthy balance.

3. *"Interns should be baptized believers, students at Ole Miss, and members of the Church of Christ."* Interns were undergraduate student leaders. Many of them had come from a Church of Christ background over the years but we had a few leaders that we excluded because of this rule. They were hurt by our rule and sometimes left the ministry. I know we can't be home to every student, but I felt like we were missing an opportunity to show them what it's like to serve in our church tradition. Maybe long-term they would have found their way into a healthy Church of Christ. I would have preferred a little more flexibility in this area of student leadership, but I understood that it made things messy and more complicated. Again, have an honest conversation with your leadership about this.

4. *"Provide leadership that mobilizes the OCOC membership in its support of the campus ministry program, facilitates intergenerational relationships, and integrates the campus ministry program with other OCOC activities and initiatives."* In other words, we wanted RFC and OCOC to be connected and have a healthy flourishing relationship. I longed for this too and over the years, we saw it happen with things like our Haiti work and the prayer room. But I did not see this as something I could make happen. I'm sure this was partly a flaw in my leadership that I didn't see how to strategically help this happen. I also knew that what we wanted took time, should happen organically and would happen with varying degrees of success because the student group was always changing. Prayerfully consider how you would address this issue.

5. *"Maintain active relationships with peer campus ministers to stay abreast of effective strategies for dealing with students."* I included this one because of how well I was connected with my peer campus ministers through the annual conference. Ironically, I believe they informed many of my views that the elders saw differently from me.

This is hard to quantify, but I will caution you and your leadership on how working agreements are used. Much of it is necessary in our legal world and boundaries are important for both ministers and elders so that they can function harmoniously together. There is, however, a tipping point where the detail included in the agreement can become overwhelming and hard to implement. I felt like I was at that tipping point.

Carlus Gupton

Though there were many good things still happening with students, it was a hard year under the microscope. Living like you are under constant evaluation is a hard way to live. Almost daily, I wrestled with if I had done things in such a way that my elders would be pleased. At some point, I had to tell God that I was doing the best I could and trust him with the outcomes. Thankfully, God sent Carlus Gupton to be our interim preacher after Lendy's move. He quickly became a good friend and guide through this process.

As we were coming up on a year under the new working agreement, there were still plenty of concerns and no talk of reestablishing the apprenticeship. Carlus was still hopeful as indicated in this text to me in **April 2018:** *"I woke up this morning feeling strong in the Spirit and with steadfastness of hope. This blessing from God always stirs me with holy imagination and creativity. I am thankful for the opportunity to serve you and the OCOC elders as I go into tonight's meeting. I will be at the table with gracious, godly men. You are his strong servant, and I am honored to come alongside you."* Carlus was in the difficult position of trying to meld my vision and the elder's vision into something workable for both of us but thankfully, God had equipped him to be a non-anxious mediator between us. Here are some comments he included as we reworked my working agreement yet again:

> *We will operate with the understanding that it is unrealistic to expect adjustments to every concern expressed by members and will strive to filter and process the feedback that is most important to the mission, maturation, and ministry of those served.*
>
> *We will maintain openness to legitimate feedback, with the understanding that frequent evaluative comments are often difficult to process and can be demoralizing and counterproductive. We will follow a fair, standardized, and periodic means of assessment, as this is usually more effective in the long run.*

These statements were much appreciated by me because church members and/or elders were providing regular feedback that was often hard to hear or process in the moment. I was trying to keep five plates spinning, but someone else was focused on a different five. It felt like we had set up a customer feedback box and everyone wanted to put in their two cents.

After this, Carlus got the elders to clarify their biggest concerns and got me to write goals that tried to address their concerns. Here was one of their concerns:

Assume primary up-front leadership of the campus ministry as a whole and secondary development of apprentices and interns.

So, my goals focused on:

- Working more closely with interns,
- Getting students in our church small groups,
- Going to counseling to strengthen my leadership skills.

I know "up-front" was an important word to my elders. I wish I had asked them more about what those words meant, but this seemed to be a big clue as to how my leadership style differed from what they preferred. I already thought I was "up-front" in many ways and I certainly was more by not having apprentices. Still, we all agreed to the new working agreement and I went into the fall a little more hopeful. I gave this testimony about Carlus: *"Having worked with Carlus for over a year, I firmly believe God used him to help our church family and my ministry through a transition he helped us to name as a 'wilderness period.' It wasn't always easy and was actually quite challenging at times, but I knew Carlus wanted to do what was best for us given our cultural context, history, and theological beliefs. He came to Oxford a lot, we emailed often, had zoom conference calls and even talked late at night a few times. He has set us up for a season of fruitfulness filled with hope!"*

I really thought we were over the hump and better days were ahead. I was right, but not in the way I had hoped.

Reflect

- *What change in my working agreement resonated the most with you and why? How would you define your leadership style?*

50

Death of a Saint

April 2012: *"I was not here the Sunday you preached on the Holy Spirit. I have just finished listening to that sermon. Thank you for your excellent exposition of what the New Testament teaches about how the Spirit lives and functions within us. Your lesson has given me a new awareness of the indwelling of the Spirit and the blessings that His indwelling affords me. Thank you and please keep up your study and teaching."* Doug Sr.

March 2017: *"Doug Sr. told Trace that he wished he was going to be around for the next 25 years. I wish he was too."*

On July 31st, 2018, I sent Doug Sr. a picture of us at the conference at Auburn and invited him to donate for the year. He was one of my annual donors to the vision I had cast back in 2015 to raise support for apprentices and interns. Of course, I was honored that the man God had used to start the campus ministry in 1960 was financially willing to support the vision God had given me. For some reason, I don't recall ever going to Doug with my troubles. Maybe I didn't want to bother him, but I think it was more that it didn't feel right venting my frustrations to him. A month later, this kind yet tenacious Jesus-following southern gentleman died on September 1st. Here was part of his obituary:

"At the University of Mississippi…he served more than 40 years as a Professor of Physics, Associate Dean of the School of Liberal Arts, and as a Founding Scientist of the National Center for Physical Acoustics. However, his primary endeavors in life revolved around his family and the kingdom of God, which he saw clearly as the

Lord's church. At an early age, his mentors convinced him that a Christian should make life decisions with kingdom goals in mind. Convinced that a public university was an important venue for the gospel message, he moved to Oxford to teach at Ole Miss in 1959. He served the Oxford church of Christ from then until his passing as a teacher, deacon, elder, and encourager. Cora Beal was his full partner in this ministry and together they used their home, offering hospitality to small and great. Doug and Cora Beal worked with other zealous Christians to establish the University Christian Student Center in 1960, and that ministry continues today under the direction of the Oxford church of Christ as the 'Rebels for Christ.'"

Doug's funeral was a celebration of a life well lived. He had been so clearly devoted to his family, the local church, and the greater kingdom work done through campus ministry. There was even a stunning rainbow on the day of his funeral seeming to indicate that even creation itself was celebrating Doug's life and that God was keeping his promise to see Doug through to his eternal reward.

First, it was the death of Lendy's ministry in Oxford. Second, it was Elza's declining health and eventual death that had taken Eric's shepherd support out of my day-to-day ministry. Now, the man who had told Kenny to do whatever it took to hire me, the man who had supported me so well for 14 years was gone. It's just a simple, painful fact that death changes things. I see now that God was at work in it, but I didn't realize at the time that the death of Lendy's ministry and these saints would create ripple effects that meant death for me as well.

Reflect

- *What stands out to you about Doug's life and vision? How have you seen the death of a beloved supporter or family member change the dynamics of your life or ministry?*

- ***Respond:*** *Practice writing your obituary. What would you want to be remembered for? Now see if your present activities are taking you in that direction.*

51

My Chinese Brother

"We...will confine our boasting to the sphere of service God himself has assigned to us, a sphere that also includes you." 2 Corinthians 10:13

I was connected with a Chinese man, Ryan, in May 2015. Ryan's wife taught Chinese on campus, but it was very difficult for him to get a job because of the type of visa he had. But this made it easier for him to meet to work on his English. We started with the FriendSpeak Luke workbook, and I'm sure we progressed through several others like John and Acts. Again, it was most weeks for an hour, usually at his home. Here is something I wrote in my journal:

> *"Meeting with Ryan was great but challenging. He said that before our study he believed in the Bible 15%. Now he said it's 70%. Still has lots of challenges but his faith is growing. He did say it was a miracle perhaps from God that his landlord gave him 4 months free rent due to problems with his house. Lord, help him believe!"*

It was neat to see some kind of measurable growth from his perspective. Over time I got to do what Paul described in 1 Thessalonians—not only share the gospel, but our lives as well. Here are some ways I was able to walk alongside Ryan.

- He had car trouble, so I helped him find a mechanic.
- He had some accidents in his car, so I helped him deal with his insurance company. Our international friends often feel the need to drive but don't have the experience needed. Unfortunately, sometimes Americans can also take advantage of our international friends, so it helps them to have an American advocate.

- He and his wife had a son and I helped them get connected with Tracey's doctors.
- I helped him save $300 on one of his medical bills and that gave him some peace of mind. I was certainly no stranger to medical bills and insurance hassles after all Tracey had been through so God was using that so I could serve him.
- We had his family over to our house for a few meals.

Here were a few things that happened along the way:

- In February 2017, I wrote this: *"He said he told his wife about his desire to become a Christian which was huge. She is not supportive at this point."* He talked about the "miracles" in his life that show God cares about him. I was proud of him for sharing his faith with his wife and hurt for him that she was not supportive.
- In April 2017, Ryan emailed these precious words: "I will pray for Tracey" because of her hospital struggles. I was very encouraged that someone who had not yet committed their life to Jesus was willing to pray. I took this as a great sign. I responded with, *"Thank you so much for praying for Tracey. I hope Jesus and Christianity will continue to be attractive to you as you read and search for what is true and right."*
- There was at least once, maybe twice, when Ryan went back to China, and I wasn't sure if I would ever see him again.
- There were weeks when I wasn't sure we were getting anywhere spiritually.
- There were weeks when he asked great questions, and I knew he was thinking about what the Bible said.
- We occasionally talked about commitment to Jesus in baptism, but I was careful not to push too hard.
- He and his family began to attend the Chinese worship service on Friday nights.

After more than three years of meeting and not meeting, serving him, studying with him, and nudging him, Ryan committed his life to Jesus in baptism just a few weeks after Doug Sr. died. My journal summed it up perfectly: *"3 years of friendship became brotherhood."* Looking back, it seemed like redemption for my time getting cut short with my Chinese friend, David, back in 2005-2006. With enough love, prayer, and time, our friends will see the beauty of Jesus and give their lives to him.

Sometimes we plant and water and see God give the increase and sometimes we don't. We have to trust that he will keep working. In 2022, I had befriended 20+ Chinese students who now had to return home. I was faced with a really heavy question as I stared at the Bible I wanted to give them: what do you tell someone you might never see again? Here's what I wrote:

"Dear friend,

Everything we did was out of love for you and Jesus. I am so glad we became friends this year and made some great memories. I hope and pray I will see you again in this life or the next one. We will always be friends, but I hope someday you will be my sister. Find out how in this Bible.

Blessings,

Casey

Christmas 2022"

Reflect

- *How have you seen God at work in an international friendship? What are some ways you have and can continue to serve them?*

- ***Resource****: The Gospel Goes to College Volume 1 has two chapters on international ministry.*

52

The Reluctant Evangelist

"For Christ's love compels us..." 2 Corinthians 5:14

As I mentioned back in my "Afraid of Evangelism" chapter, I have always had a strained relationship with evangelism. Internally, you can see from my story that I felt the heartburn that comes from knowing Jesus and feeling compelled to share. Externally, I was critiqued in my growth reviews and in other settings that I needed to be more evangelistic. I enjoyed teaching a Bible class or preaching where it was mostly followers of Jesus and a few seekers. But it still felt too safe. There is a marvelous line at the end of a wonderful book called *The Shaping of Things to Come* where the author quotes Paulo Coelho: "The ship is safest when it's in port. But that's not what ships were made for." This hit me deep in my soul. It was actually Jim Brinkerhoff who put me onto *The Shaping of Things to Come*. I quoted him in May 2010: *"How are we going to reach our children and grandchildren in a culture where Christ is progressively marginalized? I can tell you this...It's not going to happen by trying to keep them/us safe! The future of Christ in America holds no place for Christians who are withdrawn and nominal."* You could hear him wrestling with the safety that too many of us Christians had grown up in and were now too scared to leave because ships are safest in port. I took the risk every year of flying to Haiti despite my fear of flying. I also suffered physically and emotionally in many ways for the students and the Haitians, but I always knew it was worth it. I took the risk of starting a support team asking friends and alumni to financially support my ministry as we trained interns and apprentices. What could be scarier than asking people for money? So why was I not willing to take the risk of sharing my faith? I knew well the verses mentioned above from 2 Corinthians. I did want to persuade others. I did feel compelled by Christ to a point. I knew I was an ambassador for Christ in many ways but as an evangelist? We had done outreach events on campus and engaged students with free hugs and questions about Jesus and the church. That was the closest I ever felt to being an evangelist. I still had this nagging feeling I wasn't fully living into the evangelistic vision God had for my life. I cannot emphasize two things enough. First, I believe it was God's Holy Spirit living in me that was softly and tenderly trying to grow me as a disciple of Jesus. Second, it has to be one of Satan's biggest schemes to do everything within his power to keep us from sharing our faith.

In 2012, I wrote down some simple insights from my former campus minister Scott. He was on furlough from Ireland. As someone who was doing mission work in post-Christian Europe, he gave me a glimpse into where mission work in America was headed. Even though these words are brief, I understand them even better ten years later:

1. He spends a lot of time around the lost.
2. Petty vs. important conversations
3. Would the American church allow Scott to do here what he does there in Ireland?

I didn't spend much time around the lost. Once I did everything that was "needed" for my ministry, there wasn't much time left for direct contact with lost students. I also tried hard not to get caught up in petty conversations. I wanted to have important conversations that mattered with students. I found myself wanting to take the conversation deeper. And the American church—there's plenty of stats you can find. You know the news in general isn't good. Would my church allow me to spend my time similarly to a missionary in Europe? Hard to say. I wish I had found ways to ask my leadership more about how I spent my time.

In 2014, I journaled this:

"Father, thank you for opening my eyes to the void of evangelism in my life. I see at least 3 personal barriers.

1. Fear of rejection and afraid of what others will think of me
2. No real practical Holy Spirit living/ working in us
3. Was not modeled by our formative teachers"

Everyone who struggles to share their faith has fear, right? Maybe it was tied to being an introvert or the fact that I was a thinker and reflector more than a doer. I didn't get a lot of training in evangelism growing up at home or in the church. The biggest thing I did was invite someone to a youth event or worship service which is still important and can be life-changing. But is that all there is to evangelism? I still remember the time Stan Granberg, former Executive Director of *Kairos Church Planting*, modeled evangelism for me at a restaurant in Memphis. He asked our waitress if there was anything we could pray about for her. That seemed like a simple, gentle but powerful way to enter someone's life and gauge their spiritual interest. I imagined going up to someone asking, "Hey what can I be praying for you today?" and I could feel the awkwardness in my gut. When I actually did it, I could see the surprise or shock on their faces. I learned over time with lots of feeble attempts that it wasn't about me. The fear was irrational just like my fear of flying. I discovered that most people would share a prayer request if they weren't in a big rush. Plus, I learned to imagine what my worst-case scenario was—that people would look at me weird or ignore me or laugh at me with their friends as I walked away. That's it. Maybe a few folks have had it worse. However, given the persecution that many Christians around the world experience for their faith, including death, I remind myself as often as possible that this small discomfort I feel when sharing my faith is the least I can do to honor the resurrected Lord and his people suffering around the world.

I continued in my journal:

"Then you showed me at least 3 corporate/systemic barriers.

1. *We no longer have a plan.*
2. *The Boston movement hurt us, and we fear to repeat their mistakes.*[62]
3. *Christian schools are training pastors/teachers, not evangelists."*

I grew up regularly hearing the "Plan of Salvation," as we called it, which involved five steps: Hear, Believe, Repent, Confess, and Be Baptized.[63] This

---

[62] "Churches of Christ have a traditionally poor base north and east of the Bible belt. During the peak of the Crossroads movement in the late 1970s, Churches of Christ had several strong ministries at universities in Maryland, New Jersey, Ohio, and so on. As Crossroads became the Boston church and their tactics became openly aggressive and manipulative, Church of Christ campus ministries under Boston control were eventually banned at campuses such as the University of Maryland, Boston University, etc. Many churches split or lost members, and the result was especially devastating for our outreach to young people in the mid-Atlantic and Northeast regions. The campus ministries at WVU and Virginia Tech survived (barely), but the momentum of the 1970s had vanished." Jason Locke, *National Campus Ministry Seminar Conference Notebook*, 2004.

[63] M. Eugene Boring, *Disciples and the Bible: A History of Disciples Biblical Interpretation in North America*, St. Louis: Chalice Press, 1997, 396-400.

plan was a summation of the conversion stories in Acts plus things Paul said in his letters. I was certainly not opposed to these steps but felt like the process of sharing wasn't organic and it seemed to strip the biblical story of some of its power. Plus, the students I wanted to reach weren't immediately ready for the five steps. My Chinese brother, Ryan, heard those "steps" after months and years of reading the Bible. Many of the American students I worked with who came from different faith backgrounds already believed those "steps" just in a different order or with a different emphasis. I felt like the big issue was that we had not adapted and formed a new plan. In my time at Ole Miss, I never came up with a different plan that I felt good about. I did invest in a few students as Milton had taught me and that was beginning to bear some fruit. Second, because the Boston Movement had originated on college campuses, we were overly cautious about how we did evangelism on our campuses.[64] Universities were on the lookout for groups that were evangelistic in ways that could be interpreted or misinterpreted as manipulative and coercive. You had to be careful how you went about it. Finally, even with my great experience at ACU, it felt like I had been trained to be a pastor/teacher of existing Christians way more than as an evangelist of the lost.

I concluded with this prayer:

"God it's one thing to understand. It's another thing to do something about it. Help me, whether I have the gift or not to become a better evangelist. Please use me! I think you have trained me and given me the kind of personality that could do godly evangelism."

"Whether I have the gift or not" was an important phrase to me. I knew from Ephesians 4 that the Spirit did gift some disciples to be evangelists. I know there are a few gifted evangelists out there. But I didn't feel like I had the gift. Instead, Milton helped me focus on Colossians 4:2-6.

"Devote yourselves to prayer, being watchful and thankful. And pray for us, too, that God may open a door for our message, so that we may proclaim the mystery of Christ, for which I am in chains. Pray that I may proclaim it clearly, as I should. Be wise in the way you act toward outsiders; make the most of every opportunity. Let your conversation be always full of grace, seasoned with salt, so that you may know how to answer everyone."

---

[64] For further historical exploration on this movement, see Richard T. Hughes, *Reviving the Ancient Faith: The Story of Churches of Christ in America*, Grand Rapids: Eerdmans, 1996, 357-363.

In my message I know I made this point—Paul was not speaking to the evangelists in the church. He was speaking to the church. Everyone can devote themselves to prayer. Everyone can be watchful and thankful. Everyone can be wise and make the most of opportunities. Everyone can have gracious, salty words to share with whomever they meet. With the Spirit's help, everyone can be a *reluctant evangelist*. I also noted that when I prayed before going out to share my faith, it was much easier. When I was with at least one other disciple, it was even easier. After the fifth or tenth time asking someone—even easier. *Prayer, partnership, and practice were a great combination for sharing faith.*

I can think of no better way to end this chapter than with the words of Jesus in Luke 15. *"Then Jesus told them this parable: 'Suppose one of you has a hundred sheep and loses one of them. Doesn't he leave the ninety-nine in the open country and go after the lost sheep until he finds it? And when he finds it, he joyfully puts it on his shoulders and goes home. Then he calls his friends and neighbors together and says, "Rejoice with me; I have found my lost sheep." I tell you that in the same way, there will be more rejoicing in heaven over one sinner who repents than over ninety-nine righteous persons who do not need to repent."*[65]

The ninety-nine sheep remind me of our safe campus and church gatherings. May Jesus' words challenge our churches, campus ministries, and all of you reluctant evangelists out there who hear the Spirit's whispers and sense that it's time for your ship to leave port. Of course, Christians still need to repent too, and I felt like I was repenting of my fear every time I shared my faith.

Reflect

- *What have been your feelings and practical experiences with evangelism?*

- ***Respond:*** *Ask a stranger if there's anything you can pray about for them and see what happens.*

---

[65] Luke 15:3-7

53

Soul Care

"Praise be to…the God of all comfort, who comforts us in all our troubles so that we can comfort those in any trouble…" 2 Corinthians 1:3-4

"Frodo wouldn't have got far without Sam." The Lord of the Rings

In November 2018, God gave me the soul care I needed to strengthen and sustain me through my trials. Kevin Wooten, long-time campus minister at Kentucky, had been doing a mentoring group for years with a group of campus ministers and was looking to start another group. Our group consisted of a great group of guys including my former apprentice, Dalton. We met at a beautiful cabin in the middle of nowhere Kentucky. We went on a very cold hike together along the nearby river. Two of us at a time would pick a meal to prepare together. We had large blocks of time where we shared about ourselves—how we were doing, our key relationships, our frustrations, and our dreams. We shared a resource that had blessed us in the last year. In our final session, we ended with each of us sharing a prayer of the heart that our fellow campus ministers would commit to pray for the next 12 months. Everyone had stuff to share, good and bad. It was so cathartic and healing to go around the room and hear everyone talk about their ministries. I enjoyed escaping from some of my troubles and entering their stories. We laughed a good bit and shed a few tears. But at some point, everyone's story would resonate with my own and the sadness and anxiety would creep back in. I shared a lot about my struggles. I tried my best to honor my elders, but I was in a safe place and knew I didn't have to get every word just right. I don't know how I would have kept going without an oasis like this in my ministry wilderness. The Spirit, through Kevin and my fellow campus ministers, had given me a great gift—the gift of love and acceptance, safely sharing my life with those who understood campus ministry best. The greatest gift they gave me was the ability to keep going, to endure a little longer, while I waited for God to bring about some kind of resolution.

Reflect

- *Who has God given you to encourage you when you needed it most?*

54

God Still Uses Voicemail

Let me refresh your memory on my relationship with Rusty Jordan.

1. Rusty and I first connected at the 2015 conference when he first entered campus ministry.
2. Then we got to know each other better at the 2016 fall retreat in Virginia.
3. He had called me about once a year since 2015 to discuss some ministry ideas.

I liked Rusty's discipleship emphasis and the vision he was creating in Delaware.

As the new year began, Rusty called me on January 11th, 2019, and left this voicemail:

"We have decided to go ahead with the transition that I've been talking to you about. As of this year, my new role is Director of Campus Missions. With that, we are looking for somebody who is discipleship focused who is wanting to come on long-term to work alongside of me running the local campus ministry aspect of things. And I was wondering if I could send you the job description and if you know anybody who you think might fit into the role, contact me over the next few weeks."

Discipleship focused, long-term work, local campus ministry. I was glad to know of this opportunity and I'm sure I let the rest of the Campus for Christ Board know. Honestly, I didn't think much of it at the time. I was preparing for another trip to Gulf Coast Getaway. But God was preparing me for something I wasn't quite ready to see.

Reflect

- *How was God preparing you for something you weren't quite ready to see?*

55

Microcosm

"Make room for us in your hearts. We have wronged no one, we have corrupted no one, we have exploited no one." 2 Corinthians 7:2

Microcosm: a situation regarded as encapsulating in miniature the characteristic qualities or features of something much larger.[66]

I recall driving with my family to Panama City Beach for the 2019 Gulf Coast Getaway (GCG). Reed helped to drive the church van full of students to Florida. Reed is Dale's son and helped with the international ministry. There were years when I had driven the church van and was able to again if needed, but I thought it would be okay to delegate this to Reed since he was willing and able.

While there we encountered some trouble with the church van. I got a call from Reed that it wouldn't start. We had all finished lunch, and I was heading back to the condo with my family. As soon as I dropped them off, I headed back to deal with the church van. It wasn't cranking for some reason. From this point on, I was fully invested in locating a mechanic, figuring out what part was needed, and working with Reed to get the issue fixed. I know we had to jump or tow the church van hoping it would be fixed by Monday morning when the students needed to head back.

Sunday morning after the worship session, we all had lunch. Both of our campus ministry shepherd couples had come down to participate and see what GCG was like. I believe Dale and his wife had been the previous year,

---

[66] https://search.yahoo.com/search?fr=mcafee&type=E210US714G0&p=microcosm

but this was Jim and his wife's first trip. They seemed to have an enjoyable time and I thought it was great for them to get this first-hand experience at an event that had been such a great catalyst for ministry and missions in the spring semester. After lunch, they headed back to Oxford. I continued to work on the church van issue as needed and thankfully, it was ready to go by Monday morning.

On Sunday night, after the final session, all the RFCs gathered and we had a special time of reflection on the weekend. I remember Olivia, one of our student interns, encouraging us to go around the room and affirm one another in some way. I remember affirming some of our international students for stepping out in faith just by coming on the trip. Most of them were not yet believers in Jesus so it was a big deal that they had come. I remember several of the students, American and International, affirming me for inviting them, welcoming them, and helping them feel like part of our community. It was a really special time together and I went to bed like I had so many times before, content and feeling like I was doing what I was supposed to be doing.

I saw the students off on Monday, but our family stayed another day so that I could unwind a little bit and enjoy more time with my family. GCG was a perfect example of the struggle to juggle ministry and family. Tracey was a trooper juggling the kids. I helped as much as I could, but she knew most of my time was focused on the students from Friday night to Sunday night. And from my point of view, I invested a lot in students during that time, especially during the worship sessions, meals, late-night devotionals, and hangouts on the beach.

Now you would think that a little detail like my shepherds heading back to Oxford Sunday afternoon and missing the evening's fellowship wouldn't be a big deal. Turns out—it was. Soon after my return to Oxford, I got feedback that my not going back with the students and taking that extra day to be with family was not the kind of leadership that was expected of me. To quote my working agreement, I was not leading "up-front." From my perspective, I was juggling my family and the students as best I could and was doing an honorable job at it.

I think what hurt the most was that I could not seem to get it right with my elders. After all the meetings and good-faith attempts I had made to adapt per my working agreement, it felt like I kept missing the mark. I'm sure from their perspective they were frustrated that I was not adapting the way they had hoped. Remember that letter from Kenny back in 2007 when he compared me to his son? *"Your heart, Casey, is much like that and I want to respect the gifts God has given you and work with you."* I felt like my heart was not being seen, that the gifts I brought to the table were not being taken into account, and I was not being treated as a partner in ministry to work with, but someone who was simply supposed to do what they were told. After almost 15 years in ministry at Ole Miss, I felt I deserved better than that. It felt like this was a different view of leadership that was being asked of me, but it wasn't my style nor had it been my habit any of the previous years. Again, I confess this is how I felt at the time. I'm not saying all my feelings were accurate. Likely, my repetitive incompetence in some areas caused the elders to lose trust in me to manage my ministry the way I always had, and we couldn't find that sweet spot where we got back in sync. I had learned to juggle family and ministry the best way I knew how, and you now know why. Tracey and I had missed those early months with Miles and then we had persevered so long waiting to see Maggie and Moses enter the world. The fact that I had missed the mark yet again with some of my elders left me very unsettled. The fact that Dale and Jim had missed out on the encouraging time I had with students on Sunday night left me disoriented and wishing they had been there. Was I a competent campus minister? I was getting different answers from students and my leadership. I knew something had to give soon. I couldn't continue to live like this. The dam was about to break.

Reflect

- *What is a microcosm of your ministry or family or church life that describes an ongoing struggle you faced?*

56

The Death of My Ministry

"To the one we are an aroma that brings death; to the other, an aroma that brings life. And who is equal to such a task?" 2 Corinthians 2:16

"'No, they never end as tales,' said Frodo. 'But the people in them come and go when their part's ended. Our part will end later—or sooner.'"
The Lord of the Rings

After the voicemail, Rusty and I spoke in detail about the Delaware position on January 28, 2019, so he could give me more information to pass along to the Campus for Christ Board. On January 29th, I met with all the elders minus Eric who was traveling. I left the meeting discouraged. On February 1st, I let Rusty know by text that I would personally like to know more about the position. It just so happened that the Delaware position required fundraising, but I didn't even flinch when Rusty told me. God had started training me five years earlier to raise financial support for my ministry and now this skill allowed me to consider a position I would have otherwise dismissed.

On February 5th, I realized I was at a crossroads:

"I have had major ministry changes. Eric and Lendy are out. No apprentices. I feel like I do more ministry than ever and yet it doesn't feel like it's enough or enough of the right kind of ministry for my elders. I love them and appreciate them, but it feels like we are on different pages.

"I had a meeting with them last week. Gave them a lot of info, and they asked a few questions about growth and conflict. I was not affirmed or encouraged. That sent me

on a mission to talk with my mentors. I have been granted peace by God to leave the outcome to him, but I am again on a journey to find him and his will for me in all this. I have great hope that somehow, I will be allowed to stay and keep working here, but I can see the possibility that moving could be better for me and my family. I can see God working it out to stay or I can see him opening new and exciting doors for me to go. I am excited to see what God does and am feeling my grip lessen that I have to control this or fix this."

Providentially, this was the YouVersion verse of the day on February 5th: *"See, I am doing a new thing! Now it springs up; do you not perceive it? I am making a way in the wilderness and streams in the wasteland." (Isaiah 43:19)* I wrote these words with it: *"This was the scripture of the day when Eric met with the elders to discuss my ministry. He said the mood was such that this was the beginning of the end. This verse seemed to confirm it. Help me to trust you, Lord!"* I remember telling myself multiple times, "God is not freaking out." I knew that God was not wringing his hands, anxious about what was happening and saying, "Oh no, I can't believe this is happening to Casey." I knew God was at work and these thoughts were a relief valve for my heart when the anxiety and grief became overwhelming.

On February 7th, I emailed those who had walked with me in some way or another through the past 18 months. This is part of what I sent them: *"I am excited and scared about one option--the University of Delaware with Rusty Jordan. He and I have texted a bunch and spoke for over an hour today. There are a ton of things to like about this possibility...more of a team approach, ministers seen as partners with elders, discipleship over attraction. But it is daunting to consider leaving the South and family. I know many of you have had to make similar decisions. Tracey's parents moved to Oxford to be with us a couple of years ago. They are praying and aware now, but we are unsure if they would follow us. I need your help to consider other options if God is calling us to consider something else. My first conference was in West Virginia in 2004 and we prayed for the Northeast. Maybe God is finally answering that prayer. Two of my former apprentices are nearby in Virginia and North Carolina and Delaware does a retreat with them each fall. I spoke at the retreat a couple of years ago. A lot of things seem to be pointing this way so please help slow me down if I need to consider something else."*

On February 13th, I taught my last Wednesday night lesson for the RFCs. I didn't know it would be my last lesson going into it, though I knew the end was near. After visiting with students for a bit, my two campus elders asked to meet me in my office—my office of 15 years. We had had so many meetings in the last 18 months. Most of them were unpleasant. My anxiety tended to spike with each new meeting. But I knew this one would be different. We sat down and they handed me a piece of paper. They wanted me to read it, so I sat quietly and began to read. Here is what it said (slightly condensed):

"Over the last 18 months or so, it has become painfully evident that changes needed to be made in the RFC campus ministry. During that time, the elders have agonized over what to do, what would help, and how we could better serve the cause of Christ on the Ole Miss campus. We have had many discussions and shed many tears, but the result is we feel it best for RFC to go in a different direction and for you to discontinue your role as Campus Minister.

"Please know that we do not place the responsibility for the difficulties at RFC solely on you. We acknowledge our shortcomings in understanding some of the variables in your ministry. We acknowledge our failures in communication and finding common ground. We confess struggling with knowing how to establish coherency between the church and the student ministry instead of migrating into different stage life groups. We struggle with the many tensions of mission versus edification, personal agendas versus ministerial direction, and the shortfalls of human weakness. However, there is an inadequacy in our team effort that we feel would best be addressed by a fresh start for all concerned.

"Casey, you are a highly gifted man with a passionate drive to be of service to others. We know there are people serving in campus ministry because of your drive to plant campus ministries across the USA. We affirm your giftedness of care for hurting people by establishing the Back Yard Missions and your attention to the Haitians through RFC. Even though by nature you are a non-confrontational person, you have stepped up to meet with people who have a grievance against you. We know of your faithfulness to prayer and your prayer walks. We avow that your love for reaching the students is true and heartfelt. Because we affirm your gifts, and because we affirm the difficulties that will be placed on your family during this time, and because we love and value you, we would like to offer you a temporary position/opportunity.

"Should you voluntarily resign, we are prepared to help you make a lateral move to OCOC for at least twelve and potentially up to 18 months. Assuming this new role would provide a lengthy transition time and would afford you the opportunity to comfortably seek and secure a new ministry or direction for your family. Also, as should be expected in these situations, we would expect you to work alongside us in maintaining positive interactions concerning your transition with OCOC and RFC, to make this time as redemptive as possible for everyone involved. We pray that this transition time will allow for healing, growth, and even greater kingdom service."

What a note! I am glad they wrote it down for me so I could remember everything. Some of you might have preferred your elders just speak from the heart but I think you can see the many layers involved and why this way was so helpful to me.

Let me talk about several of the layers here.

First, I know many ministers have had it way worse than me. They were not honored in any way when they were fired or asked to resign though they had done nothing wrong morally. They were not given a temporary position and they were not affirmed for the good they brought to the ministry. My shepherds honored and affirmed me in several ways as you can see, and I truly thank them for that. I can see and hear their hearts in these words. I am glad they agonized over it. Every eldership should agonize over whether to retain or dismiss a minister. I am glad they shed tears. I know that means they loved me and my family, despite my incompetence. I loved them too and still do.

Second, you can see that our relationship had gotten too complicated. All the meetings, all the changes to the working agreement, all the normal ministry tensions like balancing church and campus priorities just got to be too much. It honestly felt like a relationship where you try and make it work but you can never get on the same page. At some point, the merciful thing is to end it.

Third, having never done this before, I was naïve about the process of resigning. By Sunday, I had written a short note informing the congregation that I was resigning. I shared it with the elders and Carlus beforehand. Dale got up after me and said a few kind words. Many were shocked of course. One thing we had not taken into account was that the congregation would think this "resigning" was all my idea. Tracey heard someone tell her afterward, "I hope y'all find what you're looking for." We immediately realized that the decision sounded like it came totally from us, which it obviously had not. We were in a pinch trying to honor the elders' request to maintain positive interactions but feeling like we couldn't share the truth as to how this had come about. We met with the elders within a week to explain our struggle and they thankfully permitted us to acknowledge that my resignation was at the elders' request. We had been by each other's side through years of messy, challenging situations. It was just hard to be on the receiving end this time. I know for several weeks Tracey made sure people understood it was at the elders' request that we were leaving, and I was honored that she stood up for me and wanted our church family to understand the situation better. Eventually, we had to accept that some people might not get the whole story. We couldn't make things better anymore. This is the point you have to get to—to accept that it really is the end of your ministry and there's nothing you can do to save it.

Of course, God's work at Ole Miss would continue without me which is in itself a humbling reality. Alas, John the Baptist and Eric were right again— I am not the Messiah. I know that the work God did through me was not in vain. Many students, church members, and neighbors in Oxford got to see Jesus imperfectly through me and God's work in them continues in some small way because of me. I knew deep down that God was going to keep working through me and my family somewhere else. But my heart and gut told a different story: the day-to-day work with those students in that Student Center on that campus in that city was over. My part in God's tale at Ole Miss had come to an end.

Reflect

- *What stood out to you in the elders' letter to me? What do you remember about the death of your ministry, losing a job or losing a dear minister in your life?*

57

The Aftermath

"Sorrowful, yet always rejoicing." 2 Corinthians 6:10

On February 15th, this verse of the day spoke to the death I was experiencing as my ministry had been slowly dying since that day back in 2017 when I learned there would be no more apprentices. *"Though the fig tree does not bud and there are no grapes on the vines, though the olive crop fails and the fields produce no food, though there are no sheep in the pen and no cattle in the stalls, yet I will rejoice in the Lord, I will be joyful in God my Savior." Habakkuk 3:17*

In the aftermath of this slow death, I have asked myself many times, "Where did I go wrong? What could I have done to save my ministry? God, why didn't you stop this?" There's a great story in Acts 15 about Paul and Barnabas that helps me. I've always considered myself like Barnabas—a son of encouragement. He was also the brave soul who went to Tarsus to look for Saul and bring him to Antioch in Acts 11. I like to think of myself as a scaredy-cat who can be brave when it really counts. Then from Acts 13-15, Paul and Barnabas are mentioned together about ten times like some well-known duo you know. It sounds like they are joined at the hip as they go about doing the mission of God. By the end of Acts 15, Paul wants them to go back and visit all the believers they had helped bring to Jesus and see how they were doing. It was a mission of encouragement. I'm sure Barnabas was excited, except he wanted to bring Mark along, but Paul did not think it wise since he had deserted them previously. The Bible says they had a "sharp disagreement" and "parted company." Barnabas took Mark and went in one direction while Paul took Silas and went in another. It must have been terribly sad and painful. But Luke shows us that even a sharp disagreement between brothers multiplied the kingdom's work as one mission trip became two. Paul represented my Oxford elders, and I was Barnabas. We had done mission work together for fifteen years. We were joined at the hip. But I wanted to take along apprentices, and they did not. We had a sharp disagreement and parted company. (By the way, "sharp disagreement" does not have to mean arguing and shouting. It was a peaceful but painful discussion between me and the elders.) The church stayed put and eventually hired their Silas, a great young campus minister, Ben Brinkerhoff, son of Jim and Mary. I left in search of a church that was willing to let me mentor a Mark. Sometimes there are major doctrinal disagreements or moral failures that cause churches and ministers to part ways, but that was not the case this time. This time, our kingdom visions and preferred leadership styles for reaching the campus were just different.

In the aftermath of my resignation, I was blessed to receive so many texts of encouragement. I'm sure they kept me sane, but I had a knot in my stomach and chest pain for months as I dealt with the grief that accompanied the death of my ministry at Ole Miss. These two were sweet and sad:

"I never once thought you all would not be here when Miles, Maggie, and Moses grew up...Just when it seemed the road was smooth, off you go to Delaware. Seriously? Did you have to go so far?" Tommie (church member)

"I can't believe that I am writing these words to you right now. I have put writing this letter off for so many emotional reasons. I honestly can't believe y'all are leaving after 15 years of service at OCOC." Laura (Doug Sr.'s granddaughter)

Then there was Jessica. We had served together in Haiti; she had helped with the coffee house and lots more. She was a woman on a mission with God and I took her encouragement deep into my hurting heart: *"Hey Casey I don't know what's going on, but you truly care about your students and have ALWAYS been a huge encouragement to me personally. Me and my mom both cried. So proud of you!"*

What a blessing for Jessica to encourage me after all my years of seeking to encourage her. Other students chimed in as well:

"Your role at RFC had a profound impact on me and many others. Your family was the very first thing that made Oxford home for me—and I'll always remember and cherish that. Your love is apparent and abundant and I'm sorry about everything." Camille

"I want you to know that what you did and have done for RFC and the students here at Ole Miss was not done in vain and will not go to waste. I'm thankful I got the chance to work with you and find my passions in ministry with your guiding hand as an advocate for me and so many other women." Hannah G.

Several parents sent heartfelt encouragement but this one sums it up best: *"Thank you so much for all that you and your family have done for Bailey. I don't know you very well, but Bailey tells me you are the type of person that makes people feel welcome and wanted. That was exactly what she needed when she started at Ole Miss two years ago. She did not know anyone, and the adjustment was not easy. She has always felt welcome and comfortable with RFC. You are great at what you do, and we wish you all the best at your new job."* Glenna and family

I was also comforted to receive a text from Anne, daughter of Doug Shields Sr. Her connection to Doug made whatever she had to say special to me. I hoped to hear his voice through hers.

"Just felt called to touch base with you this morning and say some things to you that I know my dad would want to say to you. I know that you don't know me that well, but my dad just loved you so much that I couldn't let this opportunity pass. I think he would say that the last chapter has not been written. That the kingdom is so much bigger than we can imagine. That God's love for us and the church is so overwhelming that despite the church's many flaws and misguided intentions we never should give up on one another. He would say that the student center belongs to Jesus. He would say that you are gifted (something he actually did say about you to me). And that you and Tracey's servant hearts are destined for many great things in the upside-down way God has of bringing hearts into his kingdom and changing the old crusty ones already defending it."

I did hear Doug's voice. I still get choked up that he saw the Student Center and the campus ministry as belonging to Jesus. It was a bittersweet reminder that it didn't belong to me either. As much as I would have wanted Doug to protest the elders' decision (I like to think he would have), he would have submitted and accepted that the kingdom was bigger than me or him. And that meant a lot coming from the man who had the vision for campus ministry at Ole Miss.

This is what death does—it triggers those treasured memories we don't think about until death arrives at our door. Our minds pull out these sacred stories: when we first met, and special moments we shared like a trip to Haiti. We remember that time we laughed about something stupid I said in a Bible study. We remember that time we cried when a student lost their grandparent or even a parent. And then we reflect on what it all meant. But there's a dark side to the aftermath of death. It causes doubt and confusion. It's the Saturday between Good Friday and Easter Sunday. Jesus knew this when he told the disciples, "You do not realize now what I am doing, but later you will understand."[67] Several times since 2017 I had wondered: Should I be a campus minister? Have I become ineffective? Am I too old to work with students anymore? In the light of day, these aren't rational questions and that's the point. When you've experienced the slow decline of your ministry for almost two years until it finally ends, it is easy in the aftermath to doubt yourself and question God.

Reflect

- *What "aftermath" have you experienced in a relationship whether in a church or personal setting.*

---

[67] John 13:7

58

Hall of Discipleship

"You yourselves are our letter, written on our hearts, known and read by everyone." 2 Corinthians 3:2

I marvel at the stories told about a loved one after they die. As I mentioned earlier, the death itself triggers years of memories that are still in our heads and hearts but were not accessed until the loved one died. In light of this, the death of my ministry caused me to go back and seek out memories from my 15 years in Oxford. I realized that it was time with Jesus and time with students one-on-one and in small groups that really mattered. It was the same with my church family. As Milton had taught me back at the 2009 conference, I continue to realize how much time I spent on circles 4, 5, and 6 planning and executing events, teaching, and preaching for large groups. Again, none of this is bad. I just think it was out of balance. But in the end, what has left the greatest impression on me, and I hope on RFC students, OCOC, Haitians, and anyone else, is the relationships—the work done in circles 1, 2, and 3.

This chapter is a tribute to all the work done over the years to make disciples. It is a little long so you may prefer to skim but I'll still invite you to get comfortable, take your time, and soak it in so you can see the many moments that make up a campus minister's life. Any minister would have similar stories. If Hebrews 11 is a hall of faith, then consider this chapter a hall of discipleship. Looking back, there are always regrets. I wish I had invested in a few students more consistently because the Spirit and I could have taken them further. I know I jumped around too much, trying to spin too many plates at one time. I hope you will forgive me, students. I am sorry that my vision wasn't more focused. This tribute is in the spirit of Paul's words quoted above from 2 Corinthians. The people mentioned below are my letters of recommendation wherever I go.[68]

May 2007: *"Thank you again and again for your support and spiritual instruction. Your marriage is our model."*

January 2008: *"Someone called me on Christmas Eve desperate and suicidal. Kelcy and I took her to get treatment. (She was baptized into Jesus, March 2008.)"*

May 2009: *"Another semester is gone. We've had a good time with Jonathan the last few days. I feel a hole inside thinking about him leaving."*

July 2010: *"Had a powerful prayer time with John today before he moved to Jackson. He teared up feeling the weight of his memories and leaving Oxford."*

October 2010: *"James was baptized on Saturday in the Mississippi River. James is the first student to be baptized through our ministry. Thank you, God! It took 6.5 years but I'm thankful."*

July 2011: *"The new school year with new freshmen is on my mind and heart. I can only imagine how much time and energy this ministry requires from you and Tracey. Y'all are a bright light for the Lord. And you for all the time you invested into Jon and I personally. You and Lendy mean so much to us both."*

March 2012: *"I asked a new freshman this spring to share a little about what brought her to us. The night she came she was choking up and feeling 'lost' when she talked to Tracey and Kelcy. Here is what she wrote: 'I came to RFC because I was really starting to feel kind of a presence of the devil in my life and I needed a refuge to help get my life back on track. I really wanted to go to RFC all last semester. I'm trying to find some people to be friends with and watch my back because I know I'm not very strong against temptations and bad influences.'"*

August 2012: *"Andrew and Megan (Soup) were married today. In February 2011, they came to our house for an emergency meeting. Megan was tempted to run away from the relationship as there was fear about the future. Megan was sure about missions and Andrew was unsure. We said you weren't going to find a guy like Andrew and that they needed to see how things went in Haiti."*

November 2012: *"Thankfully God sent Ben (a student) to minister to us tonight with a complete meal! He fixed chicken spaghetti, brought salad and cookies. It was*

---

[68] If I quote a student, it will most often be anonymous due to the personal nature of some comments.

a great moment to see God provide for us in that way. It was perfect timing (we were struggling with the twins)."

February 2012: *"Put off baptism for years...roommates' death and GCG led me to the water one year ago. I want to thank you for everything you did to help me reach my decision."*

April 2013: *"Late in the day a young man came in and started playing our piano (at the Student Center). Clearly upset, he broke down almost immediately and started saying he was gay but didn't want to be. Still in shock, I listened then took him out to courtyard. He left in better spirits, and I felt like God used me to show him love. Don't know if I'll ever see him again...I did the best I could to love, learn, and listen."*

May 2013: *"I just want to tell you thank you for providing a safe haven for young adults at the student center. The atmosphere was so refreshing to me while I was at Ole Miss. It's so difficult to continue to do the right thing while being away from your parents for the first time and surrounded by worldliness. I didn't have to worry about that at least twice a week at the Student Center."*

June 2013: *"I wanted to thank you for your comment about the student and coffee in the auditorium. I have never said a word to anyone about having coffee or whatever in the auditorium. However, I have certainly 'judged' such behavior (and others) in my head/heart. Thank you for a reminder that things are not always as they seem and to keep my mind and heart open to look beyond appearances and actions of any type."*

September 2013: *"This past Wednesday night I was thankful I could share the word of God about Jesus with the leper. But the word caused a student to discover and unleash some feelings he had been hiding and suppressing. He talked about many things from his disabled brother to cutting wood with an axe and thinking he could hurt himself. One girl even confessed to attempting suicide a while back. They felt the social isolation of the leper—made me realize how deadly it can be."*

November 2013: *"Nick texted saying he was proposing and asked us to pray."*

February 2014: *"My First Skeptic. Southern Baptist background. Considers herself a witch. Believes Jesus was real—not sure what to do about him. She is sweet, kind, skeptical, inquisitive.*

March 2014: *"A dad texted this last night: 'I prayed years ago that God would send someone to influence my boys to seek him and his ways. Thank you for your influence.'"*

"If you have any free time, I really would like to talk to you about your decision to get into ministry. I have been getting a feeling like God might be calling me to something other than football."

November 2014: *"Text from student about her roommate: She used to have faith but believed God wasn't there when she got raped."*

"I wanted to tell you thank you for the lesson tonight. I have been extremely anxious lately because my parents are getting divorced, and it has truly thrown me for a spin. You know how homesick I get during the school year and the fact that I no longer have a home there to go back to has truly been making me anxious and making me worry constantly. I truly needed your words tonight more than you could know."

March 2015: *"I met a student today. I just wanted to pass along that…she is especially fond of and feels connected to RFC. She talked about how welcome she feels every time she attends an RFC meeting/function, and she thinks highly of you, Claire, and Deonte. Thought you might like to hear how much of an incredible impact you're having on the Ole Miss community!"*

March 2015: *"A mom told her freshman chemical engineering son he couldn't be a preacher/minister because teachers are judged more harshly (James 3)."*

May 2015: *"Had supper with student. His girlfriend had lost her brother to suicide, and she was struggling mightily. He texted 'just keep praying for her. I'm really worried about her and it's almost to the point where only God can handle it. So I pray that he does. Thanks for today, Casey. It really meant a lot.'"*

"Brother Casey, I want to change my heart. That's not impossible, is it? I bet God doesn't like the fact that I need to start over every few days or so. I'm very sincere but for some reason, I fall back down. Brother Casey, please pray for me when you find the time. I can feel your prayers working but I'd be lying if I said I'm 100% where I need to be with the Lord."

December 2015: *"So thankful for the freshmen and leadership who came out to the house last night. It's certainly a perk of campus ministry to have your kids grow up around college students."*

October 2016: *"Hey Casey I'm very thankful for the relationship we have and that you're somebody I can confess to and trust in. You have really impacted my spiritual* *life and have made me a better person and come closer to God. You're a great minister and I know you'll continue to impact people like you have me."*

November 2016: *"Just wanted to thank you for everything you do with RFC. I know I haven't shared a ton of my spiritual background with you but being able to worship in a stable church environment the last 4 years has been a massive blessing. OCOC is a special place, you and Lendy have changed the way I view a lot of things. Not sure I realized the impact of it until I returned to my home church for the first time in 4 years this past week."*

December 2016: *"Last time with Chinese student today. Our conversations were the first time he had ever heard about Jesus."*

January 2017: *"I had tears in my eyes when you were talking about cynicism. I didn't know how much of it I've been holding onto. I'll be praying about it, and thanks for helping to open my eyes."*

January 2018: *"Thank you for being a wonderful spiritual leader in my life. Not just as my pastor, but as my friend and as a father figure. And for being someone I can look up to not just when you are around people, but even when you are alone. I'm very fortunate to have someone like you and your family to love and to trust."*

"I was so anxious to walk into a room where I knew no one that I actually left and went back to my apartment. Casey texted me and I explained myself and he told me to come back and he would walk in with me to make me feel safer and less anxious. And I was so thankful for Casey that night. And if he hadn't gotten me to come in, I wouldn't have met Lori and would never have met Jenna and Michelle."

February 2018: *"Your job the next sixth months: Be brainstorming possible campus ministry plants. It's an early idea and we definitely will need a lot of guidance if this is where God is leading us."*

April 2018: *"We have lost two babies to miscarriages in the last 6 months. We have always wanted a large family. I know it is very different than what y'all went through…but I knew y'all would understand this type of grief."*

June 2018: *"My parents have gotten countless compliments on how much people loved you and your message at our wedding. Got to watch the wedding video today and I couldn't agree more. We are so thankful for you, Casey."*

August 2018: *"Prayers for your strength during next week and the weeks to come. Thank you for being the ROCK for the college kids. If you have ever doubted your ministry (which I had very recently), please know that us parents have such* *faith/ comfort in your ability to lead our college students/ young adults. They are facing many new obstacles and Satan pulling them in other directions. Hang in there Casey!"*

September 2018: *"Read Mark 1 with Nepalese student yesterday in his office. It was really exciting to hear his voice reading those words."*

October 2018: *"Happy birthday Casey and thank you for being a best friend as well as a guardian for us in the city."*

Similar to what the Hebrews writer says in chapter 11, I do not have time to tell about all the other relationships and conversations that I didn't write down, but I know this gives you a glimpse of the life of a campus minister. It is humbling and glorious. I know I shared the gospel. I know I shared my life with students. I've tried to be honest about my weaknesses and faults along the way, but this was the perfect time to just look back and celebrate what God did through me in 15 years at Ole Miss.

Reflect

- *What is your impression of ministry after reading these comments?*

59

Tightrope

"I have labored and toiled and have often gone without sleep."
2 Corinthians 11:27

"So I risk it all just to be with you; And I risk it all for this life we choose."
"Tightrope," The Greatest Showman

After being asked to resign on the 13th, I had a first interview with the Delaware search committee the next day that went well. We met again the next week for a more in-depth interview. I got the message below from Rusty on March 6th and it scared me. The timing made it seem even more like God was orchestrating a move to Delaware.

"I personally referred the other guy (who interviewed for the position) as we both know him. And since November, we both thought we would be working with him and were frustrated at all the constant delays to get to the point of hiring him. I thought we would have started the hiring process in October and a decision made by the end of the year. Some of the delays were my fault, random things, etc...and 4.5 months later I was very frustrated but now believe God delayed my timetable for a reason (and I say that very, very sparingly that God caused things). We have all sorts of people praying around the world asking for God to give clarity...."

We took the whole family to Delaware for the interview weekend thanks to a supporter who helped with our kids' plane tickets. Tracey and I were convinced that if we made a move this big, we owed it to our kids to let them see Delaware before we made a decision. Not that they had veto power, but I said several times, that if we moved, we would be changing the trajectory of our kids' lives. The kinds of people they would marry, the places they might live and work—the possibilities seemed so different now. It certainly felt strange leaving the Philadelphia airport with one of the elders. The pit in my stomach told me that we might as well be in a foreign land. We were warmly greeted by the church leadership on Saturday night. I had the chance to preach on Sunday. I met with the Board of the campus ministry Sunday afternoon. I was painfully clear about some of the things I was leaving behind in Oxford and wanted to make sure the leadership had a different approach. Every indication was that the ministers took the lead in their ministries with appropriate oversight and input from the elders. No one was going to be constantly looking over my shoulder. I talked a good bit about their definition of success. It seemed to fit mine. We came home without any major red flags other than the fact it was Delaware. Now I understand how Jesus felt when people questioned "Nazareth?" Delaware seemed just as surprising. So now Tracey and I faced the difficult task of making this decision together. We were both still grieving and nursing emotional wounds. Marriage can be challenging under stable conditions, but we were in a perfect storm battling the strain that a relocation puts on a marriage and family. Even when Tracey had health issues, we knew where home was. Even when the ministry had been hard, I could come home at night, vent to Tracey and go back to work the next day. Now home could be Delaware? Near the end of March, we got the resolution we needed. Here's my journal:

"Saturday night our family watched The Greatest Showman again since we hadn't watched it in a while. At some point, I told Tracey how underrated the 'Tightrope' song was, but that it had really grown on me because of how it resonates with me and our marriage. Yesterday we received an offer from the Newark church to consider and I read it to Tracey at lunchtime. Last night, when I was about to fall asleep, Tracey got my attention and said she wanted to play me a song and that she hoped I would understand why she was playing it. She played 'Tightrope' and I knew that meant her answer to Delaware was 'yes'! I couldn't believe it but was so in awe of God's work in her heart and how humbled that she would follow me on this call to Delaware. She read a couple of old journal entries from years ago where she talked about how she wanted to be along for the ride wherever God might send us. It was beautiful and unexpected and I am praising God! Now the joy of telling others. Keep knocking down doors, Lord!"

It was a wonderful feeling but unlike the acceptance of the Ole Miss job in 2004, this one came with baggage. In all honesty, God had used the timing of the Delaware position to sustain my spirit more than I realized. Those quiet questions about whether I should be in campus ministry and whether I am a competent campus minister were quickly answered by the disciples in Delaware who wanted to hire me. Still, after we came down from the high of the interview, trip, offer, and acceptance, the hurt unexpectedly crept back in. Now I didn't have the distraction of the new job. God had parted the waters for Delaware in an amazing way. But I was still grieving the death of my ministry at Ole Miss and would be wandering in my emotional wilderness for four more months while the kids finished school and we prepared to move. It was a providential gift that God was allowing me to grieve before we left Oxford.

In June, I sent this note to my beloved soul care brothers. I was hurting and in desperate need of encouragement. *"Life has been crazy. I am struggling in the transition. We are getting our house on the market this week. I'm trying to raise support for my new ministry and keep my interim job in Oxford. I covet your prayers for all these new adventures in our transition life. They announced here Sunday that the search committee was formed, and they would begin looking for a new campus minister...so that was weird and sad."*

Deron from Purdue sent this: *"Love you, Casey! So sorry for all the craziness. I know from experience that moving/job changes can really leave you wandering, not to mention everything else life throws your way. Know that we are here for you and God will continue to bless others through you no matter where you go or what you do. Praying for peace, strength, clarity, and a strong sense of God's love over you and your family as you go through this wilderness."*

Kevin at Kentucky sent this: *"I am praying for you and Tracey to be a solid team in this transition, for your kids to be eager for a new experience, for your house to sell and a new home to be available and affordable where you can make some great memories doing kingdom business. I am also praying that your wilderness time will not be wasted in negative thoughts or attitudes but rather a valuable time of waiting, listening, being prepared, and making a path to close a beautiful chapter of your life in Oxford. You're a good man and I am inspired by your willingness to take on a new adventure far away from the familiar. Thanks for being a model of faithfulness and trust in a sovereign God."*

I really needed those words of encouragement. I feel guilty rereading the words about not wasting time on negative thoughts. Death and grief can really cloud and darken your vision, making it hard to see and experience good things the way God intended.

P.S. Upon arrival in Delaware, I learned quickly that Darrell Swanson was the visionary for the campus ministry. He and his wife, Janet, invested many, many hours in students, especially international students over the years. They are both approaching 90 years old but are still active and supportive. It hit me while writing this story that Darrell is the Doug Sr. of Delaware. I hesitate to say it that way, but please understand I know these are two very different men, but the thing that so clearly connects them is their vision for the campus and the kingdom. Doug had a vision for Ole Miss and beyond. Darrell has a vision for UD and beyond. And they both brought the rest of us into their large campus-focused orbit. They love the campus where they have invested the most, but they always wanted other campuses to have the same blessings. We need these visionaries to help the rest of us dream a bigger kingdom dream. I hope you have someone like this in your church, but if not, maybe God is calling you to champion campus missions (or any mission)!

60

A Song of Discipleship

"As you come to him, the living Stone…you also, like living stones, are being built into a spiritual house…." 1 Peter 2:4-5

It was hard deciding what I would preach in my final sermon at the end of June. I had preached roughly once a month for 15 years. Now I had to figure out what to say in 30 minutes or less to a congregation that I dearly loved. *"I have said before that you have such a place in our hearts that we would live or die with you."*[69] I decided to preach about a song I had written back in 2007. The words of the song were based on a combination of themes drawn from 1 Peter and the idea that the church is a people not a place. Everybody has a pet peeve and as a Bible nerd, mine was theological. Early in my ministry, the thought occurred to me, "We don't go to church. We are the church." And thus, the idea for the song was born. The church is the flesh of Christ, the house and temple of God, not a bricks and mortar building. The church is on campus and in the community spreading like wildfire as it is led by the Spirit. My hope is that we can fulfill our mission to live into God's intention for us to go beyond the blessings and curses of a building to be his manifold wisdom.[70]

---

[69] 2 Corinthians 7:3
[70] Ephesians 3:10

Casey Coston

<u>Go Be the Church</u>

As we gather here on our Lord's Day
Heaven and earth collide in our hearts and minds
Empty tomb still speaks to our empty lives
Giving hope to those who are hungry
We're the flesh of Christ bonded with his blood
We're a body not a building
We're all broken parts looking to our head
Head that moves each part by his gracious will.

Supper, songs and prayer, word and water
Sacred symbols, holy rituals
Teach and save us Lord in these strange events
Make us strangers in the world for Christ
We're the house of God, we are living stones
And his house stands firm on the goodness of grace
We are his people not some hollow place
And we long for more to become a stone.

As we leave this place one thought fills our minds
Jesus could return, faith replaced by sight
Heaven and earth will meet one final time
When we fly to meet Jesus in the air.
We are God's temple, seeking holiness
And his Spirit works to fulfill that dream
"Go to church" is not our Savior's call
Now his Spirit sends us, "Go be the church."

Thanks to Melanie and no doubt others, the church gave us a lovely going away party including some generous donations for our new adventure. Though being asked to resign will certainly make someone feel like they failed,[71] it did provide some healing to be sent out in this way. I will always be grateful to the Oxford Church of Christ and the elders for that. As I mentioned earlier, I know some ministers are not treated nearly as well as I was. Melanie was able to make sure that my uncle's painting of Jesus in the

---

[71] "Though we may seem to have failed." 2 Corinthians 13:7

garden from the prayer room was also given as a gift. I was so thankful I could take it with us. Though certainly not physical life or death, I had wrestled in prayer for the life of my ministry. It was terribly symbolic. I had told God I wanted to stay, but for his will to be done. And his will was done—we didn't stay.

Reflect

- *Do you see the church as a body or a building? Why do you think that is?*

- *How have you used Jesus' garden prayer in your life?*

61

New Life in Delaware

"That is why, for Christ's sake, I delight in weaknesses, in insults, in hardships, in persecutions, in difficulties. For when I am weak, then I am strong."
2 Corinthians 12:10

"But that's not the way of it with the tales that really mattered or the ones that stay in their mind. Folk seem to have been just landed in them, usually—their paths were laid that way." The Lord of the Rings

Everything was about to change. Isaiah 42:16 was fixing to be put to the test yet again. God was certainly leading us, the blind, by ways we had not known. Were the rough places going to be made smooth? Was darkness really going to become light? In hindsight it is clear that the answer was "yes" but it wasn't clear at the time. Thankfully, God provided comfort and courage for every weak moment we faced. One huge dose of comfort came after a very long day of packing the U-Haul. I was physically hurting and irritable. Our son, Miles, had decided that he wanted to be baptized into Jesus before we moved. There is no image more revealing of death and resurrection than baptism. We gathered one last time with a few friends on a quiet Monday night at the Oxford Church of Christ. I was so thankful for how Miles connected baptism with leaving behind both his old life of sin and his old life in Mississippi. He was raised to new life in Jesus as we began our journey to a new life in Delaware. Tracey and I were so physically weary but spiritually sustained by this kind of good news.

God gave me another comfort on the day we left Oxford and began the journey to Delaware. A former student, Betsy, sent me this text:

"We are incredibly thankful for the love and support we received from you and Tracey. Jon and I were with y'all during the most tumultuous years of our relationship. Those years were certainly formative in regard to our future marriage. Those counseling sessions with you, Lendy, Jon, and I were so hard but so helpful. Those hard years set us up for what has been a truly wonderful, peaceful but imperfect marriage. My years in Oxford were often very trying and unpleasant, but my memories of y'all and the student center are all wonderful. I learned the restorative power of prayer during the early morning slots of the prayer marathons in that small room in the student center. As much as I stressed about school and had to study constantly, I eventually learned that putting time aside for God FIRST always pays metaphorical dividends in many ways. Often with peace that passes understanding. Lendy once said to me that college is a spiritual desert. It was true for me. But having such wonderful support and love from you guys helped me eventually come out the other side to an oasis."

I was grateful to know that the death of my ministry had produced this kind of reflection in Betsy. It reminded me that God was at work in all things just as he had promised in Romans 8. It meant that God worked for good even in unexpected job losses and big moves. It meant God was bringing new, resurrection life out of death.

Now I know what you're wondering—was God planning for our family to move to Delaware the whole time? Did he know at my second conversion or when I took the Ole Miss job? Did my prayer at the conference in 2004 change something? Was it the saints in Delaware who stepped out in faith to move mission mountains? I still don't have a clear answer. It is likely some mysterious combination of sovereignty and free will. Maybe some things are fixed, and some things are flexible. But the numerous nudges over the years toward the Northeast were hard to ignore:

- My first conference in West Virginia and the prayer for the Northeast
- The spring break trips to West Virginia and Maryland
- The 2013 conference in Delaware and getting *The God Ask* book
- Raising financial support in 2015
- Connecting with Rusty at the 2015 conference and staying in touch
- The trip to Maryland with Dalton and Eric
- The 2016 Fall retreat in Virginia which included Rusty and the Delaware ministry
- Two of my former apprentices were campus ministers in Virginia and North Carolina

Then there was the team approach, a partnership with the Board, Newark elders, and staff. There was a focus on discipleship and investing in a few students rather than an attraction/event-based ministry. Finally, the desire to train apprentices for new campus ministries in the Northeast was especially compelling and was like a salve on a sore spot in my soul. Whatever was unclear, I knew God had brought new life out of death. Perhaps one of the best moments of the fall semester was when we went on retreat with other ministries and Tracey took a picture of me side-by-side with Dalton and Deonte. That moment and picture meant a thousand words and more. It was concrete evidence that God had sent us to Delaware. To be sure, the fall was still very challenging for our family as we adjusted to our whole new life. Waves of guilt threatened to overwhelm me seeing my family struggle, but I knew I had done all I could to stay in Oxford. At the end of the day, I clung to the hope that God was leading us and things would get better for everyone, not just me. Now after a few years, God has proven himself faithful and blessed our family's leap of faith.

I hope you caught on that I intentionally wove verses from 2 Corinthians into my story. Every morning before I began writing this book in the summer of 2022, I would meditate on portions of Paul's letter to sharpen my axe. Nowhere else do I find such phrases that draw me in and resonate with my experience as a campus minister, husband, and father. Paul felt like he had been sentenced to death. So did Tracey and I with her health troubles and our pursuit of more children. "Hard pressed but not crushed"—an ancient version of our athletic phrase "bend but don't break." Ministry and life had pressed me very hard, but I had not been crushed. But the one that means the most is, "For when I am weak, then I am strong."[72] His power made perfect in my weaknesses. All the insecurities produced in the last two years at Ole Miss drove me to prayer walks with the only One with whom I felt completely safe and secure. All the inadequacies revealed during growth reviews and meetings with the elders forced me to lean on God to make me strong and competent as a minister of the gospel. I don't think I've ever boasted about it like Paul, but regardless, God did his part because this is how his kingdom works. I want you to see that for Paul, death and resurrection were woven into his story and that meant he was living in God's story. Please check out **Appendix B** to see how Paul wove death and resurrection into 2 Corinthians.

---

[72] 2 Corinthians 12:10

Death and resurrection are threaded through my story as well. On a large scale, I could not have experienced new life in Delaware if my ministry at Ole Miss hadn't ended. The irony of death and resurrection is that something has to end for something new to begin; something has to die for something new to grow. As hard as things were at Ole Miss, it had become too difficult to find the right combination of parameters that would work for everyone. Only in hindsight can I see the grace God was giving me to let my ministry die so I could start again. But there were lots of little things on a smaller scale too. My near burnout (death) had led to solitude and prayer walks (resurrection). Growth reviews (death) had led to growth (resurrection). Tracey's health struggles (death) had led to endurance and a marriage refined by fire (resurrection). I was particularly saddened that I could no longer care for and watch the trees I had planted for my wife and kids grow. But I planted new trees for them at our home in Newark and now watch them grow. Someday, I hope far in the future, there will be death here in Delaware, but God will provide new life again. As much as we would prefer to go around death, the only way to resurrection is through it. I'm not sure I'll ever get used to dying, but I promised in my baptism to die to self for the rest of my life. I hope I will learn better to trust that in every little death I must die along the way, new resurrection life is certainly waiting for me no matter how long it takes.

While in college, I heard a strange song coming out of my campus minister's office. It sounded like the musician was singing about Job—the man in the Old Testament. Turns out, he was. Michael Card did, in fact, write an amazing and haunting nine-minute song about the story of Job. You should check it out. It was unlike any Christian music I had ever heard. From that day on, I bought every CD (yes, I'm old) that he produced. I'll end this chapter with some lyrics from his song entitled, "God's Own Fool," because Michael mentions the mystery of the weak becoming strong. The invitation to "come be a fool as well" is an invitation to trust that God is bringing new life out of death—even if it means looking like a fool moving to Delaware.

When we in our foolishness thought we were wise
He played the fool and He opened our eyes

When we in our weakness believed we were strong
He became helpless to show we were wrong
And so we follow God's own fool
For only the foolish can tell-
Believe the unbelievable
And come be a fool as well[73]

P.S. "Hey Casey, I just wanted to let you know that I am encouraged and challenged by your choice to leave the stability of the Bible Belt to serve in the Northeast." Michael

Reflect

- *Where do you see death and resurrection being woven through the story of your life and ministry?*

---

[73] Complete lyrics: https://genius.com/Michael-card-gods-own-fool-lyrics

62

Invitation to Discipleship

"Besides everything else, I face daily the pressure of my concern for all the churches." 2 Corinthians 11:28

When we think about some of our favorite stories from the gospels, we normally think of people. The woman at the well; the woman caught in adultery; the dad who said, "I do believe, help my unbelief;" the demon-possessed man returned to his right mind; Zacchaeus; Nicodemus; and the two on the road to Emmaus. Most of these Jesus only invested in for a few moments or hours, but it was life-changing. Then consider the disciples (which is just a fancy word for "students"). He invested in these few, these twelve for a few years. Sound familiar? That's what campus ministers have—a few years with college students. How do we make the most of our time?

After 15 years in Oxford, Delaware was an opportunity for a reset and a chance to do some things differently based on the wisdom I had gained. Thankfully, Rusty made the reset easy because God had already been aligning his vision for the work at UD with what I spent most of my time doing in my final years at Ole Miss. I want to give a brief overview of my vision for the work here in Delaware with three qualifiers. First, some of you may be more naturally gifted at planning and executing events than I am. I don't want to discourage you but caution you to remember Milton's words: "Discipleship only occurs in circles 1, 2, and 3." If you start to get a nagging feeling that what you spend a lot of time on isn't helping students get closer to Jesus, reset and put the focus back on one-on-one and small group conversations. I mentioned this earlier: Events were made for students, not students for events. (It works for many things! Our phones were made for people, not people for phones.) Jesus was warning us how even good things can enslave us and become bad things if done with the wrong priorities. In other words, our loves can get out of order. If we love events more than people, our ministry is not going to function the way Jesus intended. Second, we still do some attractive events here, but they are secondary and serve a larger purpose. We do a great waffle event every fall and spring thanks to a shepherd couple in our church, but we use it to help us meet students that we can follow up with for the rest of the semester. Try and use your events to create opportunities for follow-up and future conversations. Third, we don't have a lot of students with a Church of Christ background or even Christian students in general. This is a big difference between RFC and BHC, but I believe it's where most of our ministries are headed in the years to come. I don't have easy answers for those of you who are still blessed with larger ministries. I will just challenge you like I did in a previous chapter to remember Luke 15— God leaves the ninety-nine to go find the one.

The Vision

Blue Hens for Christ will be a training center to reach the nation and the nations. It's just like my RFC vision that we started in 2015 as I began raising support for the ministry. Apprentices and University of Delaware (UD) disciples will be trained to follow Jesus for the purpose of:

1. Seeking American and International students,
2. Helping students consider Jesus,
3. Teaching students to follow Jesus.

Instead of adding through events, we want to multiply through discipleship. As indicated in the 2 Timothy 2:2 verse, there is a discipleship progression:

Paul => Timothy => Reliable people => Others.[74]

The hardest part of our mission is not making disciples. *It's making disciples who will themselves, make disciples.* That's the mystery of multiplication.

---

[74] "And the things you have heard me say in the presence of many witnesses entrust to reliable people who will also be qualified to teach others." 2 Timothy 2:2

Find Your Starting Point A

One of the things I have wrestled with the most is how to meet and connect with new students besides our few attraction events. I want to look for opportunities that are more organic and rely on authenticity and felt needs more than some cool factor which I don't have. Scott Lambert taught me about pathways because these help us get from A to B. We know B is getting people to encounter Jesus through friendship, the Bible, community, prayer, etc. So, what is our starting point A? Let me share two major and two minor starting points I'm focused on that I think make a great starting point "A." You may certainly discover others that fit your context better. (There are also divine appointments waiting for us at coffee shops, prayer walking, etc.)

1. *English conversations with international students.* The great thing about international students is their desire for friendship and to improve their English. This makes it fairly easy for the love of Christ in us to intersect their desires. I mentioned before our partners in the kingdom Let's Start Talking (LST) and their American ministry "FriendSpeak."[75] They are a great resource, but we also use Easy-to-Read Bibles and start reading with our international friends directly from those. We have several ways to meet internationals here. Pray and seek the internationals on your campus then look for opportunities to invite these students into deeper conversations about the Bible while helping them improve their English. Paul said it well in Romans 15:20: *"It has always been my ambition to preach the gospel where Christ was not known so that I would not be building on someone else's foundation."* There is something very appealing about this and I think we should take Paul's missionary strategy more seriously and give more of our focus to international students.

2. *A mental health support group.* Thanks to a coaching session with *Mission Alive*, they helped me come up with the idea of a support group. We have made a great connection with a non-profit off campus called Sean's House which is focused on mental health. They have included our support group called "Unburden" in their programming (https://seanshousesl24.com/support-groups-and-programming/). They host us every two weeks. We get teens and college students regularly. You might be able to connect with counseling services on

---

[75] https://lst.org/

your campus. We also offer a support group within our ministry as a way to care for those already connected to us. We know mental health is a huge issue in our culture and it will be an ongoing issue in college for the foreseeable future. Lendy gave me a tool years ago that makes it easy for me to facilitate these groups. In fact, with just a little practice, anyone can facilitate. These are not exclusively for American students, but we do think they will be particularly interested in them. I have included more info on this in **Appendix C** if you are interested in starting a support group. Support groups function like our English conversations because they meet a felt need and give us a starting point A to care for these students and show them the love of Jesus.

3. I mentioned this earlier, but I think the Tim Keller podcast "Questioning Christianity" is going to be very useful with seekers and skeptics.

4. My dear friend, Hannah Parmelee, created this curriculum called *Relationship IQ* that I also think would work great with students. There are six modules including ones on friendship, sex, and "How to Date the Best." These could work great in any setting but consider reaching out to Greek life on your campus. Check out an overview here: https://boonecenter.pepperdine.edu/relationship-iq/get-to-know/program-overview.htm

Getting from A to B

So, what do we do once we make a connection? How do we take students from A to B? Through some of his reading and experience, Rusty showed me how conversations can go through an organic process like this:

casual => meaningful =>spiritual => biblical

I was already doing this but now I had the language and intentionality I needed to do it better. How does this play out?

Casual conversations: sports, weather, food, hobbies, movies, books, etc. (I look for connections here that naturally lead to meaningful or even spiritual conversations. For example, if a student likes a movie, it's not hard for me to get there by simply asking, "What did you like about the movie?")

Meaningful conversations: What's your major? What kind of career are you looking at? Why did you decide that? Tell me about your family. How's your mental health?

Spiritual conversations: What can I be praying for you? Share spiritual article or podcast (like "Questioning Christianity") or news that gets into the realm of God, justice, meaning, morals, etc.

Biblical conversations: Would you be willing to study the Bible with me? I usually start in a gospel so that students get a good picture of Jesus. But there are good models out there for starting in Genesis and working through a few critical stories before getting to Jesus. I really like to take students through The Bible Project's "How to Read the Bible" video series as well.

Sometimes the relationship stays casual for weeks before any meaningful things happen. Sometimes I can go from casual to Biblical in the course of one or two meetings. Every student's context is unique! When I do get to weekly one-on-one meetings, I focus on hearing their story, taking notes and trying to ask good follow-up questions. Everyone has a story, and it is cool to see how the Spirit teaches me through their story.

Investing in 8-10 Students

How do we keep up with the students we are investing in? We use an intentionality chart to help us identify roughly where students are at in their spiritual journey. This is also very helpful for our prayers. See **Appendix D**. The chart is categorized like this:

1. I usually have quite a few students in the casual/meaningful categories. (Let's say 10-20 students depending on the time of year.)
2. Then I have a few students I am meeting with for meaningful/spiritual conversations, prayerfully hoping for them to become Bible studies at some point. (Let's say 3 students weekly.)
3. Then I have seekers (2-3 weekly) and disciples (2-3 weekly) in biblical conversations.

Rusty helped me settle on approximately eight weekly relationships to invest in. Jesus had twelve and maybe someday I'll get there, but 8-10 is what I can do really well right now.

Let me give you two examples of how this played out for me. One is international and the second is American.

1) International student
    *   **Casual**: responded to our Thanksgiving sign in front of the campus house, we picked him up and he celebrated the holiday with us.

- **Meaningful**: We texted a good bit through December and January. I served him when he needed a ride to work, and we had lots of good conversations.
- **Spiritual**: We talked about faith and even went on some prayer walks together.
- **Biblical**: By April and May he was open to studying the Bible together. By August he decided he was ready to give his life to Jesus in baptism and we continue to meet most weeks, and he is eager to help others find Jesus.

2) American student
- **Casual**: Added him on Instagram when I saw he was a freshman coming to UD in 2020. Invited him to our outdoor waffle night during Covid but learned he was at home and online for the fall semester.
- **Meaningful**: Had a few conversations online about school and the pandemic.
- **Spiritual**: I didn't know if he had faith, but I prayed and asked him what I could be praying about for him, and he shared some things. We didn't appear to message again for <u>six months</u>. But then he sent me a message responding to my Instagram story about Tuesday night's Dinner and Discussion. He agreed to meet me a few days after that.
- **Biblical**: He started coming regularly to our Tuesday night gatherings. We met several times during his sophomore year, and he brought his roommate. Now they are living upstairs at the campus house and I'm inviting them to grow in Christ.

Facilitator or Expert?

One final tip that I'm still learning is adapting to the *role of facilitator more than expert*. *Mission Alive* can help train you better for this through their Discipleship Cohorts. At Ole Miss, I functioned almost exclusively as the expert. Through teaching and preaching, I was counted on to bring the right answer. Even in small groups, if a student asked me a question, I simply tried to give them the answer because I was the expert. It can make you feel important—too important. But it doesn't help nearly as much with Jesus' mission to make disciples. (Plus, sometimes experts are wrong, and students aren't always looking for experts even when they think they are. What they really want is a safe place to work out their faith in light of the Bible.) Jesus didn't always give answers, did he? He often answered a question with a question. He facilitated learning in that way. Parables weren't told to give clear answers but to get people thinking about kingdom life. So now I try to facilitate learning more through questions. I give shorter lessons and focus on discussion using the Discovery Bible Study (DBS) method.[76] Students help facilitate our discussion groups. When someone looks to me for an answer, I try to respond with a question instead. (I'm still working on this because I like being the expert!) We also do a DBS in our one-on-one studies. This helps students think for themselves and most importantly, *allows the Holy Spirit to be the teacher, not me.*

I hope this gives you a better understanding of how we connect with students, meeting them wherever they are but intentionally, slowly, lovingly, and prayerfully seeking to go deeper. *Like anything, a process based on love and prayer can morph into something legalistic, manipulative and unhealthy.* I hope you can see that these conversations take time and look different based on the student and their previous experience and needs. So now my definition of success is unapologetically focused on planting and watering like Paul said. The number I focus on now is 8-10 students weekly (with casual/meaningful outreach to several others) so I can patiently and lovingly show them Jesus. *All other numbers are not that important to me.* See **Appendix E** for my weekly schedule. I train apprentices the same way. You will need more staff to reach more students because I've learned the hard way that one person cannot effectively disciple 40-50 students. I hope from my story you can see how life-changing and liberating this is. Ultimately, this chapter is an invitation to discipleship— to lay down your life for Jesus and to invest in a few students and staff wherever you are and take them as far as you can.

Reflect

- *What stands out to you in this vision to invest in a few?*

- ***Resource:*** *Contagious Disciple Making by David and Paul Watson*

- ***Respond:*** *Begin to bring focus to your ministry by identifying the eight to ten students/people you want to focus on the most.*

---

[76] For the DBS template, check this out: https://www.dbsguide.org/

63

Closing the Loop

"We say the circuit (loop) is open when there is a gap somewhere; the electricity doesn't flow. The circuit is closed when everything is connected."[77]

I n my "Equipped…Kind Of" chapter I mentioned some exciting changes in the works that give us the chance to address some gaps in my training. Thankfully, God has been at work closing the loop. In the spring of 2022, we made this announcement to our Campus for Christ network:

*"**Campus Ministry Connections** (CMC) is a new program of Harding University, scheduled to launch in the fall of 2022. CMC is designed to do two things:*

1. *Facilitate peer-to-peer ministry/discipleship to Harding undergraduate students.*
2. *To help CMC interns prepare for public university campus ministry after graduation.*

Chris Buxton, the new CMC director, said that in the past, many ministry-minded students at Christian universities were never introduced to campus ministry as a vocational option. So, his goal with CMC is to create an 'on-ramp' for Christian university students to enter state university campus ministry. He is currently hiring up to 10 student interns who will serve under his direction as the leaders of the CMC ministry.

Another goal for the CMC program is to create relationships with campus ministries that have apprenticeship programs to receive HU graduates after they graduate. So, if your ministry is interested in becoming a partner ministry to provide CMC graduates

---

[77] https://english.stackexchange.com/questions/301527/meaning-of-phrase-to-close-the-loop-on-this/301613#301613

with apprentice or graduate internships, please send a message to chris@ulifeconsulting.org.

But wait there's more! Chris, along with the help of several others like Milton…also started a certificate program in campus ministry at Lipscomb University on the graduate level. Students can complete a nine-hour certificate program or combine four certificates for a master's degree to grow their ministry skills in any six areas of study shown on the website.[78] "

This is a wonderful pathway God has created through Chris that begins to address a missing component of my training at ACU. We now have an opportunity to change the narrative for the better—new stories will be written in student's lives that include classroom training plus practical apprenticeships. This gives future campus ministers a chance to start more equipped and competent than I was. Though there will always be personal and ministry challenges no matter how much training you receive, you can be better trained to address them. I am thankful for Chris' endurance in campus ministry and that God is now using him in this way to raise up a new generation of campus ministers. And if you are a student in one of these programs or thinking about campus ministry at all, check out our list of apprenticeships here.[79]

There's one other important way we can close the loop. Someday I hope to replace myself with an apprentice that I have trained so that kingdom work can continue uninterrupted on the Delaware campus without me. I seem to recall Jesus doing the same thing. I think this is a humble way to accept our finiteness in this kingdom story, honor God's mission to campus, and model discipleship to the next generation.

Reflect and Respond

- *If you are a full-time minister, what is the most rewarding part of it to you?*

- *If you are considering ministry, what sounds like the most rewarding thing about it?*

- *What next steps do you sense the Spirit may be nudging you to take?*

---

[78] (https://www.lipscomb.edu/academics/programs/master-arts-christian-ministry-cbe)
[79] https://www.campusforchrist.org/apprenticeships

64

We Do Not Lose Heart

"Therefore, we do not lose heart." 2 Corinthians 4:16

"But I expect they had lots of chances, like us, of turning back, only they didn't."
The Lord of the Rings

It is surprising that God did not call me to what I was best at. If he had, I would be a musician performing on stage or teaching someone else the beauty and skill of music. Or I would be an engineer designing systems and maximizing the efficiency of processes for some oil or chemical company. I could easily argue that God made me competent through my years of practice and preparation to succeed in those fields. Both of these are honorable professions, and we need plenty of godly musicians and engineers to bless our broken world. *But he called me not to what I was best at but to what was best for his kingdom.* Let's just admit that can sound counterintuitive though it makes perfect sense in the upside-down kingdom of God. He took my incompetence in ministry and slowly made me competent, all for his glory. Are we competent when we enter college or get our first job? No. I hope this book has proved that. Are we competent when we get married or become parents? Certainly not. We are made competent over time because God believes in on-the-job training! Please understand, I still have plenty of moments and days where I feel incompetent. Me getting older and college students staying the same age will do that. I've learned most days that incompetence is not the end of the world but is actually the pathway to relying on God so that he can make me competent. Again, weak made strong—death then resurrection.

So, if you've made it this far with me, I discovered a surprising seventh reason for writing this book that I think is the best way to end our journey together. Twice, at the beginning and end of 2 Corinthians 4, Paul says "Therefore, we do not lose heart." This means we don't have to despair or give up. But what does "do not lose heart" imply? Suffering, struggle, pain, loss and more. In other words, we wouldn't be tempted to lose heart if everything was easy, fun or simple, right? So brace yourself…*deep breath*…the seventh reason for writing this book is that we must be *willing* to suffer for Jesus.

If we are willing to suffer, then it is easier to not lose heart. But suffering means that we will have to do hard things. There are many subcultures that do hard things but let's take marathon runners for example. I am in awe of them for their willingness to train and then actually run 26.2 miles in ONE race. It sounds impossible and crazy to me. Who would want to put themselves through that kind of suffering? But there are about one million people each year who run a marathon. There must be something good that comes out of the suffering, or they wouldn't do it. Dear minister or student, all humans are willing to suffer for some great purpose and you must be willing to suffer and do hard things to run the marathon of ministry. You may have read my story and thought, "Who would want to put themselves through that kind of suffering?" I hope you have seen good overcoming evil, joy surpassing sadness, and resurrection light shining even in darkness.

If we are not willing to suffer, then we will do almost anything to avoid it.[80] I know there are many reasons why we avoid suffering, but I will suggest one—our consumer culture's emphasis on comfort and cost/benefit analysis (i.e. the most benefit for the least cost) are subtle yet powerful incentives to avoid suffering. For example, when is the last time you fasted by choice? We have been trained well in this curriculum. This is likely at the heart of why some don't go into ministry and why others get out. It is too much discomfort and not enough benefit. I hesitate to say this because I have no right to tell you whether you should be in ministry or not. That really is up to you and God and your trusted mentors to discern. God can certainly use any of us outside of full-time ministry. I confess that when I've suffered, I have wanted to smack Paul upside the head for saying "light and momentary troubles."[81]

---

[80] The irony of course is that if we avoid certain actions because of the suffering involved, we will still end up suffering, just in a different way. For example, if we avoid the suffering of exercise, we will still most likely face the suffering of not taking care of our bodies.

[81] 2 Corinthians 4:17

But then I remember Paul suffered a lot, I mean A LOT and still said those words, so I know he must have considered losing heart and yet experienced the resurrection power to keep going. I may not have suffered as much as you or Paul, but now you know my story and I wanted you to see the suffering in it and hopefully, it will give you some endurance for your journey. If you're considering a life of ministry, Jesus would want you to count the cost to know if you're willing to suffer. If you have already suffered in ministry, I hope you can cling to God and keep going because the next generation of potential ministers needs to see us suffer and stay in ministry.

So, let's look at the process that gets us to not lose heart.

We suffer => God gives resurrection power => we endure => we do not lose heart => repeat

I remember when Dr. Huffard (Remember "We will never evangelize someone we fear or hate.") came to Oxford and shared with us these words from Colossians 1:11—"...*being strengthened with all power according to his glorious might so that you may have great endurance and patience....*" I remember how vividly it stood out to me that we were given the amazing power of the resurrection, but did you notice what it was used for? It was given so that we might have great endurance and patience. What do you need endurance and patience for? Suffering! Ugh! That can be confusing and disappointing!

I know God's resurrection power is occasionally used for great and amazing things. Our prayers contribute to someone's healing. The new creation at work in us brings other people to Jesus so they become a new creation. Revival occurs in a church or community. But I believe its defining quality, at least until Jesus returns, is that it helps us endure all the suffering we will face in this life. Remember Paul said that what validated his ministry was not his ability to heal or teach but his endurance in the face of suffering and hardships. "*...we commend ourselves in every way: in great endurance; in troubles, hardships and distresses....*"[82] In other words, what made his resume stand out was his sufferings and God used these to make him competent.[83] *Made competent through suffering.* When I get past the perplexing disappointment of this truth, I realize what a big deal that is. I have been given a power that helps me not give up or lose heart. After all Tracey and I have been through, this is good news. In a culture with increasing mental health struggles, that is good news. In a wounded world where we get stepped on (persecution) or

---

[82] 2 Corinthians 6:4

[83] What if we had a place on our resume for our sufferings?!

over (seen as irrelevant) because of our faith in Jesus, that is good news. In a broken church, where God works through and despite imperfect disciples (even the ones in leadership), that is very good news!

This is why I want to share with you my favorite modern-day parable—a parable of endurance.

The Unmoved Rock

Once upon a time, there was a man who was sleeping at night in his cabin when suddenly his room filled with light and the Savior appeared. The Lord told the man He had work for him to do and showed him a large rock in front of his cabin. The Lord explained that the man was to push against the rock with all his might. This the man did, day after day. For many years he toiled from sun up to sun down, his shoulders set squarely against the cold, massive surface of the unmoving rock, pushing with all his might.

Each night the man returned to his cabin sore and worn out, feeling that his whole day had been spent in vain. Seeing that the man was showing signs of discouragement, Satan decided to enter the picture placing thoughts into the man's mind such as: "You have been pushing against that rock for a long time, and it hasn't budged. Why kill yourself over this? You are never going to move it." Thus, giving the man the impression that the task was impossible and that he was a failure.

These thoughts discouraged and disheartened the man even more. "Why kill myself over this?" he thought. "I'll just put in my time, giving just the minimum of effort and that will be good enough." And that he planned to do until one day he decided to make it a matter of prayer and take his troubled thoughts to the Lord.

"Lord," he said, "I have labored long and hard in your service, putting all my strength to do that which you have asked. Yet, after all this time, I have not even budged that rock a half a millimeter. What is wrong? Why am I failing?" To this the Lord responded compassionately, "My child, when long ago I asked you to serve me and you accepted, I told you that your task was to push against the rock with all your strength, which you have done. Never once did I mention to you that I expected you to move it. Your task was to push. And now you come to me, your strength spent, thinking that you have failed. But, is that really so? Look at yourself. Your arms are strong and muscled, your back sinewed and brown, your hands are callused from constant pressure, and your legs have become

massive and hard. Through opposition, you have grown much and your abilities now surpass that which you used to have. Yet you haven't moved the rock. But your calling was to be obedient and to push and to exercise your faith and trust in My wisdom. This you have done. I, my child, will now move the rock.'[84]

I can see myself so clearly in this story. I pushed against the rock for 15 years. I was faithful to my family, my church and my ministry to Ole Miss students. I tried to figure out how to move the rock many times but all I could do was push. And in the end, God moved the rock and sent my family to Delaware where we have begun to push against the rock here. And surprise, surprise, "…what has happened to me has actually served to advance the gospel." [85]

There is always a tendency to see yourself in another person's story. Much of that is natural because that's how stories work. But I would caution you from seeing a one-to-one correspondence. Perhaps you will think it's time to get out of the ministry because of something I wrote and that's possible. Just please don't look for a secret message in my story. If anything, I hope my story will make it *less likely* for you to think it's time to move on or get out. As always, with time, prayer, waiting on the Lord, and looking to trusted mentors, things will become clearer. The Spirit will move you at just the right time…even if it hurts. I encourage you to keep pushing against whatever rock God has called you to. And for those in high school or college thinking about ministry and those in seminary preparing for ministry, I think you know deep down that the best things in life are often the hardest. Put another way, the best things in life often come with suffering built in—marriage and parenting come to mind quickly. I hope you will strongly consider adding a life in ministry to that list!

I will forever be grateful to all the trusted mentors God put in my path that I have tried to honor in these pages. There will be similarities and differences as you and the Spirit write your own uniquely incompetent story in the pages of kingdom history. I hope some of us will get to read it. I want to encourage you as a minister, as a campus minister, or as someone who is considering any ministry, to accept your incompetence, reluctantly or wholeheartedly, and not lose heart. Please keep serving students and people from all nations, seekers, skeptics, and saints wherever God calls you as he makes you competent for the campus, the community and the kingdom.

---

[84] https://bible.org/illustration/unmoved-rock
[85] Philippians 1:12

"May the grace of the Lord Jesus Christ, and the love of God, and the fellowship of the Holy Spirit be with you all." 2 Corinthians 13:14

Reflect

- *What are you willing to suffer for?*

- *How does it strike you that resurrection power is given mostly for our endurance?*

Appendix A

Points on the resurrection. Again read "Surprised by Hope" if possible.

1. Resurrection is part of evangelism. See Acts 17 (and most sermons in Acts)

2. Resurrection leads to celebratory worship and awe. See Revelation 5 and Hebrews 12

3. Resurrection gives us power and courage so that we don't do ministry out of fear. (Philippians 3:10)

4. Resurrection helps us care about the body, creation, and justice. (Romans 8)

5. Resurrection stirs our imagination. i.e. new heavens and new earth and new bodies

6. Resurrection gives me hope on my worst day.

7. Resurrection helps me accept and endure suffering. (Acts 4, Matthew 10:28)

8. Resurrection reminds us that God, not us, will make all things right.

9. Resurrection is about God's victory over his last enemy—death. So it's not so much about us though it affects us.

10. Resurrection only comes through death, denial, sacrifice. Can't avoid or go around death to get to resurrection. Must go through it.

Appendix B

Death and Resurrection in 2 Corinthians

Notice also that sometimes there are code words for death and resurrection:

1:5 "For just as we share abundantly in the sufferings of Christ (death), so also our comfort (resurrection) abounds through Christ."

1:9 "Indeed, we felt we had received the sentence of death. But this happened that we might not rely on ourselves but on God, who raises the dead."

2:14 "But thanks be to God, who always leads us as captives (death) in Christ's triumphal procession (resurrection)."

2:16 "To the one we are an aroma that brings death; to the other, an aroma that brings life."

3:18 "And we all…are being transformed into his image with ever-increasing glory (resurrection)"

4:10 "We always carry around in our body the death of Jesus, so that the life of Jesus may also be revealed in our body."

4:16-17 "Though outwardly we are wasting away (death), yet inwardly we are being renewed (resurrection) day by day. For our light and momentary troubles (death) are achieving for us an eternal glory (resurrection) that far outweighs them all."

5:1 "For we know that if the earthly tent we live in is destroyed (death), we have a building from God, an eternal house in heaven (resurrection), not built by human hands."

5:17 "Therefore, if anyone is in Christ, the new creation (resurrection) has come: the old (death) has gone, the new (resurrection) is here!"

6:10 "Sorrowful (death), yet always rejoicing (resurrection); poor (death), yet making many rich (resurrection); having nothing (death), and yet possessing everything (resurrection)."

12:10 "For when I am weak (death), then I am strong (resurrection)."

13:4 "For to be sure, he was crucified in weakness (death), yet he lives by God's power (resurrection)."

Appendix C

Mental Health as Mission

Problem: Seeking to build connections and relationships with American students to invest in their lives and draw them closer to Jesus.

Intervention: A mental health support group using the recovery tool FANOS for those with <u>mild to moderate mental and emotional health needs.</u> This will allow us to be a blessing and provide a service in a time of need for students while developing a relationship and getting to share Jesus and our faith along the way. The name of the group is UNBURDEN based on verses from **Matthew 11:28-30— "Come to be, all you who are weary and burdened, and I will give you rest...For my yoke is easy and my burden is light."**

F—Feelings like sad, mad, glad, anxious, etc. (You can find core feelings chart online.)

A—Affirm someone in your life for some way they blessed you (i.e. roommates, parents, friends)

N—Needs for self-care i.e. eat well, more sleep, exercise, friends, structure, generally <u>not</u> school deadlines

O—Own/ownership. Own not eating well, acting out of anger in unhealthy way, etc.

S—Sober minded. Are you present in this moment or are you regretting the past or worried about the future? Sometimes it helps students to think in terms of a percentage, i.e. "I am 50% or 80% sober."

Appendix D: Intentional Outreach Chart (Developed by Rusty Jordan)

Give roughly half your work week to relationships and then the other half for personal spiritual development, administration, and study for lessons you will teach.

Connecting: Casual/Meaningful Conversations

Activities: stay in weekly contact (casual texting, inviting to join you for things like joining some friends to eat, no big investment just building connections). Intentional prayer, etc.

_____   _____

_____   _____

_____   _____

Investing (4 Areas, 8 people max):
Meaningful/Spiritual Conversations

Intentionally connecting with each other on a weekly/monthly basis, getting coffee, inviting to house, intentionally spending time with and developing conversations. Goal is to move to spiritual conversations and then to study.

_____   _____

_____   _____

_____   _____

Seeking Faith: Spiritual/Biblical Conversation

_____   _____

_____   _____

_____   _____

Transform: Biblical Conversation

A baptized believer, helps them to grow with Christ as Lord and teach to obey his commands

_____   _____

_____   _____

_____   _____

Empower: Biblical Conversation

Someone who is now sharing, walk along with them. (Transform/Empower can go together)

_____   _____

_____   _____

_____   _____

Appendix E: Campus Minister Weekly Schedule

I'm going to share my Delaware schedule, which is healthier than my Ole Miss schedule (which I can't remember well anyway). At Ole Miss, my working agreement asked for 50 hours a week. Here in Delaware, I'm able to work closer to 40. Your schedule in your context could still look very different and my schedule changes some every semester, but I wanted to give you a template.

In general, Thursday and Saturday are rest and/or family days, Monday is spiritual development, and Sundays, Tuesdays, Wednesdays, and Fridays are big social and spiritual conversation days. This is where I try and connect with 8-10 students weekly. Some students are open to meeting weekly, others every two weeks, and some monthly. I work with what they are willing to give me.

Sunday: Morning Bible Class, Worship, Monthly Church Life Group, Reflect Board meetings every two months, monthly worship on campus. Meet with students that are hard to reach during the week.

Monday: Fasting and studying in UD library, working on monthly sermons, occasionally meet with a student in the afternoon, text students I would like to meet with Tuesday, Wednesday or Friday.

Tuesday: Morning prep for Tuesday night discussion, lots of invitations, meet with an apprentice, lunch with a student, discipleship community (roughly 4 students), staff meetings, dinner, and discussion in the evening

Wednesday: Administration (emails, fundraising, newsletters), 2-3 meetings with students, guys group in the evening

Thursday: Intentional day off with rare exceptions. <u>Make sure you take at least one day off a week.</u> Monthly church leadership meeting at night.

Friday: 2-3 meetings with students, especially international students, monthly game nights at campus house or other fun event

Saturday: Sabbath rest except for retreats, solitude. (Tailgating and football took up a lot more of my time at Ole Miss because it is such a big part of the culture.).

About Kharis Publishing:

Kharis Publishing, an imprint of Kharis Media LLC, is a leading Christian and inspirational book publisher based in Aurora, Chicago metropolitan area, Illinois. Kharis' dual mission is to give voice to under-represented writers (including women and first-time authors) and equip orphans in developing countries with literacy tools. That is why, for each book sold, the publisher channels some of the proceeds into providing books and computers for orphanages in developing countries so that these kids may learn to read, dream, and grow. For a limited time, Kharis Publishing is accepting unsolicited queries for nonfiction (Christian, self-help, memoirs, business, health and wellness) from qualified leaders, professionals, pastors, and ministers. Learn more at: https://kharispublishing.com/

www.ingramcontent.com/pod-product-compliance
Lightning Source LLC
Chambersburg PA
CBHW070029100426
42740CB00013B/2632